COSTA BRAVA TRAVEL GUIDE 2023

GW00771434

A Comprehensive Vacation Guide to Costa Brava: Plan Your Perfect Getaway, Discover Beaches, Culture & Delicious Spanish Cuisines with 7 Days Well Planned Itinerary Perfect for First Timers.

Patsy J. Tour

TABLE OF CONTENTS

Patsy J. Tour

A Comprehensive Vacation Guide to Costa Brava: Discover Beaches, Culture & Delicious Spanish Cuisines with 7 Days Well Planned Itinerary Perfect for First Timers.

COSTA BRAVA
Travel Guide
2023

I could feel the warm Mediterranean wind caress my face as I got off the plane at Girona-Costa Brava Airport, beckoning me into a world of limitless possibilities. I had no idea that my journey to Costa Brava would turn out to be an experience that would live on in my memories for the rest of my life. Girona, a wonderful city, was my first destination. Its historic cobblestone alleys, beautiful residences, and fascinating history immediately captivated me. I felt the weight of centuries of tales and customs as I went through the labyrinthine lanes of the Jewish Quarter, Call Jueu. Girona Cathedral's grandeur left me speechless as I ascended its towering stairs, which were rewarded with beautiful vistas of the city.

The creative ambience of Figueres, the birthplace of the great artist Salvador Dal, drew me in. I found myself in front of the enthralling Dal Theatre-Museum, a monument to Dal's singular and unconventional vision. The museum's strange exhibitions took me to a realm where imagination ruled supreme. Dal's talent could be seen in every location, from melting clocks to funny sculptures.

Tossa de Mar, a lovely village on the coast, promises peace and beauty. I spent my nights roaming through the medieval old town's twisting walkways, enthralled by the ancient walls that guarded the town's secrets. Tossa de Mar Castle rose atop the hill, guarding the beautiful Mediterranean. The sky created a symphony of hues as the sun set below the horizon, casting a magnificent spell over the town.

Cadaqués, a lovely beach resort, beckoned, offering a calm vacation. I strolled through the little lanes lined with white-washed cottages, their blue shutters standing out against the turquoise sea. A visit to the Salvador Dal House-Museum provided me with an insight into the artist's personal life as well as the inspiration that infused his works. Portlligat Bay, with its calm seas and secluded coves, was the ideal location for peaceful reflection.

The natural park of Cap de Creus, a beautiful seaside beauty, enticed me to explore its harsh terrain. I went on an exciting trek, immersing myself in the wild beauty of the cliffs and coves. The Cap de Creus Lighthouse stood majestically on the edge of the globe, directing mariners with its comforting beam. I felt a strong connection to nature with each step, its grandeur a sobering reminder of our position in the cosmos.

No trip to Costa Brava would be complete without sampling the region's gastronomic offerings. I ate typical Catalan meals including substantial seafood paella and luscious grilled prawns called gambas a la plancha. Local food markets were bursting with vivid colors and enticing fragrances, enticing me with fresh vegetables and handcrafted delicacies. And, of course, I couldn't pass up the opportunity to sample some good wine and cava, appreciating the effervescence that matched the character of the place.

My timing was fortunate as I happened across Girona's bustling Festes de Sant Narcs. Colorful parades, traditional dances, and boisterous music brought the city to life. I joined the villagers in honoring their patron saint, soaking in the festive ambiance. The sky was lighted by beautiful fireworks, which painted the night with a rainbow of hues. It was a celebration of life, community, and Costa Brava's rich cultural legacy.

Throughout my tour, I met warm-hearted residents who shared their tales, made recommendations, and welcomed me as a member of their community. Conversations flowed easily, and through their eyes, I found the genuine soul of Costa Brava. From an accidental meeting with a fisherman who taught me how to throw a net to the warm grins of café owners who gave me the perfect cup of coffee, these unexpected encounters transformed strangers into friends.

I traveled into the gorgeous Pyrenees Mountains, eager to see beyond the shore. The steep peaks and verdant valleys presented a paradise for thrill seekers. I went on exciting walks, marveling at flowing waterfalls and breathtaking views. The fresh mountain air energized me as I went mountain biking, whitewater rafting, and even paragliding. Nature welcomed me, and I felt a deep connection to the mountains' raw beauty.

As my stay in Costa Brava came to an end, I thought on the innumerable memories that had been carved into my psyche. The dynamic cities, attractive villages, breathtaking scenery, and kind people had left an everlasting imprint on my tour. Costa Brava had taught me to be open to new experiences and to enjoy the beauty of life's serendipities.

I waved goodbye to Costa Brava with a sad heart, knowing that the memories I had made would be cherished for the rest of my life. I was carrying not just mementos but also a fresh feeling of adventure and an insatiable restlessness as I boarded the aircraft back home. Costa Brava had sparked a desire in me to discover more of the world's hidden treasures, to embrace cultures, and to appreciate the friendships made along the road. In the end, my trip to Costa Brava was more than simply a holiday; it was a life-changing experience that left me with a deep respect for the beauty of life, the complexity of other cultures, and the magic that can be discovered in the most unexpected locations. Costa Brava had become a part of me, stitched into the fabric of my journeys, and I knew that one day, I would return to unravel more of its secrets and write new chapters in this never-ending saga of discovery.

Hello and welcome to Costa Brava.

Costa Brava, which translates as "Wild Coast" in Catalan, is a captivating area on Spain's northeastern coast. Costa Brava has caught the hearts of people from all over the globe with its rocky cliffs, crystal-clear seas, beautiful coastal villages, and rich cultural legacy. This is a complete introduction to this enthralling Mediterranean treasure.

Climate and Geography

Costa Brava is a 214-kilometer-long (133-mile-long) stretch of coastline in Catalonia's province of Girona. Its varied environments include beautiful beaches, secret coves, rich woods, and scenic cliffs. The area has a nice Mediterranean climate with scorching summers and moderate winters, making it an all-year resort. During the summer, the average temperature varies from 25 to 30 degrees Celsius (77 to 86 degrees Fahrenheit). Costa Brava is home to a wealth of enthralling places, each with its own distinct character. Girona's ancient buildings, cobblestone alleyways, and well-preserved Jewish Quarter attract tourists. Barcelona, although not officially part of the Costa Brava, is a vibrant town nearby that should not be overlooked, with famous attractions like as the Sagrada Familia and Park Güell. Other noteworthy locations are the gorgeous villages of Tossa de Mar, Cadaqués, Begur, and Blanes, each with its own particular personality and attractions.

Beaches & Coastal Attractions

Costa Brava's magnificent coastline, studded with a profusion of gorgeous beaches, is one of its primary charms. There is a beach for everyone, from wide sandy expanses to hidden rocky coves. There are bustling resorts in Lloret de Mar, as well as calmer choices in Sa Tuna, Tamariu, and Aiguablava. Cala Pola and Platja de Castell are secret treasures with unspoiled natural beauty. Costa Brava's beaches will capture your senses whether you want leisure, water sports, or a romantic twilight walk.

Heritage Cultural and Historical

Costa Brava is rich in history, with a plethora of cultural and historical sites awaiting discovery. Pals, with its well-preserved medieval walls and tiny lanes, transports tourists back in time. Empries' Greek and Roman remains highlight past civilizations, while the Sant Pere de Rodes Monastery provides insight into the region's religious legacy. Figueres, Salvador Dal's birthplace, is home to the Dal Theatre-Museum, a surreal masterpiece presenting the artist's works.

Nature lovers and thrill seekers will find nirvana on the Costa Brava. Natural parks in the area include Cap de Creus, Montgr, Illes Medes, and Aiguamolls de l'Empordà, which provide chances for trekking, birding, and animal observation. The Camino de Ronda coastal path is a famous route for beautiful hikes along the cliffs with amazing views of the Mediterranean Sea. Snorkeling, scuba diving, kayaking, and paddleboarding are among the water sports available.

Gastronomy and regional specialties

Costa Brava is a culinary paradise, tickling taste senses with wonderful Catalan food. Traditional foods like as paella, fideuà (a noodle dish), suquet de peix (fish stew), and botifarra amb mongetes (Catalan sausage with white beans) are available. Fresh seafood, such as prawns, squid, and anchovies, is a gastronomic highlight in the area. Drink a glass of local wine with your meal.

15 Compelling reasons why You Should visit the Costa Brava.

Costa Brava is well-known for its beautiful beaches with crystal-clear seas and stunning surroundings. There's a beach for everyone, from wide sandy stretches to quiet coves, with options for relaxation, water sports, and sunbathing.

Lovely Coastal Communities: The area is densely packed with lovely coastal communities, each with its own distinct personality and charm. Explore the historic alleyways of Tossa de Mar, the small lanes of Cadaqués, or the lively atmosphere of Lloret de Mar.

Costa Brava has a rich history and cultural heritage, with many cultural and historical places waiting to be explored. Explore ancient Greek and Roman remains at Empries, the Salvador Dal Theatre-Museum in Figueres, or Girona's well-preserved Jewish Quarter.

Outdoor Activities: Nature lovers will be spoilt for choice at Costa Brava. Several natural parks dot the landscape, providing chances for hiking, cycling, birding, and animal observation.

Discover the various ecosystems of Aiguamolls de l'Empordà or the jagged rocks of Cap de Creus.

Girona's Old Town: Girona is home to a wonderfully preserved medieval old town that is a joy to visit. Explore the city's old fortifications, small lanes lined with colorful buildings, and the majestic Girona Cathedral, which gives panoramic views of the city.

Catalan Cuisine: Foodies will revel in Costa Brava's gastronomic pleasures. Traditional Catalan delicacies such as paella, fideuà, and botifarra are served with local wines and refreshing sangria. Don't miss out on the region's fresh seafood, which includes prawns, anchovies, and squid.

The Legacy of Salvador Dal: Costa Brava is intimately identified with the great artist Salvador Dal. Explore the lovely fishing hamlet of Portlligat, where Dal lived and worked, and the Dal Theatre-Museum in Figueres, which has a large collection of his works.

Festivals and Celebrations: Festivals and celebrations capture the vivid essence of Costa Brava. From colorful street parades during Carnival to traditional Catalan holidays such as Sant Joan, these events highlight the region's rich cultural past and provide an opportunity to immerse yourself in local customs.

Wine and Cava Tasting: There are various vineyards and wineries on the Costa Brava where you may taste the region's great wines and sparkling cavas. Take a guided tour, learn about the winemaking process, and enjoy wine samples while admiring the stunning vineyard scenery.

Scenic Coastal Drives: The Costa Brava region is known for its stunning coastal drives with panoramic vistas at every bend. Take a leisurely drive over the region's meandering roads, passing past lovely villages, secluded coves, and towering cliffs. The views of the Mediterranean Sea are breathtaking.

Water Sports Adventure: Costa Brava has a variety of water sports activities for adrenaline seekers. In the region's crystal-clear waters, try your hand at snorkeling, scuba diving, kayaking, paddleboarding, or even windsurfing.

Genuine Charm of Costa Brava's Quaint Fishing communities: Discover the genuine charm of Costa Brava's quaint fishing communities. In areas like Calella de Palafrugell, Tamariu, and Palamós, you may explore the small alleyways, admire the colorful boats, and eat delicious seafood.

Cap de Creus Natural Park is a real natural beauty, distinguished by its rocky cliffs, secluded bays, and beaches.

Unique Geological Formations: The Costa Brava region is home to a variety of geological formations that will take your breath away. Visit the Aiguafreda cliffs and the famed Pont de Pedra (Stone Bridge) in Besal, an architectural masterpiece dating back to the 11th century.

Mediterranean Atmosphere and Lifestyle: Costa Brava exemplifies the laid-back Mediterranean lifestyle. Relax on the beach, enjoy a cool beverage at a coastal café, or wander along the promenades. The region's friendly residents and welcoming attitude provide a warm and appealing setting.

Costa Brava's closeness to Barcelona makes it a great option for a day trip or a longer vacation. Explore the dynamic capital city with its renowned architecture, busy markets, and exciting nightlife by taking advantage of the excellent transit links.

Coastal Hiking Paths: Put on your hiking boots and go out on coastal paths with breathtaking views of the Mediterranean Sea. The Camino de Ronda trail enables you to discover the coastline of Costa Brava, traveling through secret beaches, craggy cliffs, and attractive coastal villages.

Local Markets and Artisan Crafts: Immerse yourself in the local culture by visiting Costa Brava's lively markets. Taste fresh fruit, look at homemade goods, and talk to friendly sellers. Marketplaces such as Girona's Mercat Municipal or Palafrugell's Mercat de Palafrugell are ideal for experiencing the dynamic local atmosphere.

Wellness & Spa Retreats: Costa Brava has a variety of wellness retreats and spa resorts where you may rest and rejuvenate. Relax with luxury spa treatments, relax in thermal baths, or practice yoga in peaceful natural surroundings.

Attractions for Families: The Costa Brava offers a range of attractions and activities for families. Visit water parks like Water World in Lloret de Mar, adventure parks like Parc Aventura in Platja d'Aro, or museums like the Museu del Joguet (Toy Museum) in Figueres.

Romantic vacations: The picturesque landscapes of Costa Brava make it an ideal location for romantic vacations. Enjoy quiet meals by the sea, walk along the beach at dusk, and stay in exquisite boutique hotels in gorgeous villages.

Whether you are looking for natural beauty, cultural discovery, outdoor activities, or just relaxing by the sea, Costa Brava has a plethora of experiences that will leave an indelible impression. In this seaside paradise, embrace the region's beauty, immerse yourself in its rich past, and make amazing experiences.

Things You Should Know Before Visiting Costa Brava

Visa Requirements: Before arranging your vacation to Costa Brava, make sure you have the proper visas or travel papers to enter Spain and, if applicable, the Schengen Area.

The Euro (EUR) is the official currency in Costa Brava, as it is across Spain. Although credit cards are generally accepted, it is suggested to carry extra cash for smaller places.

Catalan is the major language spoken in Costa Brava. However, Spanish is commonly spoken as well, particularly in tourist regions. In hotels, restaurants, and tourist sites, English is widely spoken.

Peak Tourist Season: The summer months (June to August) are the busiest for tourists in Costa Brava, with many people flocking to the beaches and prominent sites. Consider going during the shoulder seasons (spring and fall) when temperatures are more pleasant and there are less people.

The weather in Costa Brava is Mediterranean, with scorching summers and moderate winters. Prepare for hot weather throughout the summer months by packing suitable attire, such as sunscreen, hats, and sunglasses.

Transportation: The Costa Brava's public transportation system is well-developed, with buses and trains linking numerous towns and attractions. Renting a vehicle might provide you greater freedom, particularly if you want to visit distant locations or go through the countryside.

Accommodation: Costa Brava has a variety of lodging alternatives, including hotels, resorts, guesthouses, and vacation rentals. To get the greatest accommodations, book ahead of time, particularly during high season.

Costa Brava is a relatively safe tourist location. However, simple measures such as keeping an eye on your valuables, avoiding secluded locations at night, and adhering to any local safety recommendations are always prudent.

Local Customs and Etiquette: Learn about the local customs and etiquette. Handshakes or kisses on both cheeks are traditional greetings. When visiting holy locations, modest dress is desirable, and it is courteous to seek permission before photographing someone.

Tipping is not required in Costa Brava, however it is common practice to round up the bill or give a little tip (about 5-10%) for excellent service in restaurants. Tipping is welcomed but not demanded for outstanding service.

Tap Water: In general, the tap water in Costa Brava is safe to drink. However, bottled water is widely accessible if you have a sensitive stomach or prefer it.

Keep in mind that certain companies, especially smaller stores and restaurants, may observe siesta hours in the afternoon, shutting for a few hours. Plan your activities and meals appropriately, and double-check the hours of operation of attractions and businesses ahead of time.

Festivals and Holidays: Throughout the year, Costa Brava celebrates several festivals, making it a colorful and exciting time to come. If you want to enjoy local customs and festivals, consult the festival schedule and plan your vacation appropriately.

Beach Etiquette: When visiting Costa Brava's beaches, be cautious of local norms and standards. Respect the environment by properly disposing of waste, and follow any safety advice given by lifeguards.

Medical Services: Costa Brava features first-rate medical facilities and hospitals. Before your journey, it is suggested that you get travel insurance that covers medical situations. Carry any required medicines with you and be familiar with emergency contact numbers.

Local food: Try traditional Catalan meals and embrace the local food. The seafood, paella, tapas, and regional delicacies of Costa Brava are well-known. Explore the local food scene by experiencing different tastes and specialities.

Respect the Environment: The Costa Brava is known for its natural beauty. Show your environmental sensitivity by engaging in responsible travel. Avoid trash, hike on approved routes, and avoid hurting or destroying any flora or animals.

Cultural Sensitivity: Respect the local culture , customs and traditions. When visiting holy places, dress modestly and keep in mind local sensitivities and social customs. To express your admiration for the local language, learn a few fundamental words in Catalan or Spanish.

Plan Ahead for famous sites: Some famous Costa Brava sites, such as the Dal Theatre-Museum in Figueres or the Girona Cathedral, may draw enormous crowds. To prevent large lines, consider purchasing tickets in advance or coming early.

Explore Beyond the Coast: While the coastal towns and beaches are beautiful, don't overlook Costa Brava's interior riches. Explore the countryside to see picturesque towns, wineries, and natural parks that provide a unique viewpoint on the area.

Stay Hydrated: During the summer, the Mediterranean temperature may be rather hot. Carry a water bottle with you and drink lots of fluids, particularly if you're doing outside activities or spending time in the sun.

Plan for a Siesta: As previously said, siesta is a prevalent habit in Spain. Some stores, especially those that are smaller, may shut for a few hours in the afternoon. Plan your activities and purchases appropriately, and keep this cultural factor in mind.

Stay Connected: In most regions, Costa Brava has strong cellphone service and Wi-Fi. To remain connected throughout your journey, consider acquiring a local SIM card or activating an international **roaming package.**

Emergency Services: Learn the local emergency phone numbers, including those for medical services, police, and the fire department. Keep these phone numbers on hand in case of an emergency.

Travel Insurance: Travel insurance that covers medical emergencies, trip cancellation, and lost or stolen possessions is highly advised. Before your vacation, review the coverage and conditions of your insurance policy.

Explore Local Markets: Costa Brava has thriving local markets where you may sample the region's genuine tastes and goods. Visit markets like Barcelona's Mercat de Sant Josep or Girona's Mercat Municipal to experience fresh vegetables, regional delicacies, and artisan crafts.

Embrace the Slow living: Costa Brava represents a peaceful and unhurried way of living. Embrace the slower pace, taste your meals, take in the scenery, and immerse yourself in the relaxed mood of the area.

By remembering these key principles, you'll be well-prepared to make the most of your vacation to Costa Brava, assuring a memorable and delightful time in this enthralling part of Spain.

Dos and Don'ts in Costa Brava

Dos:

Do respect local customs and traditions: Show respect for the local culture by being acquainted with Costa Brava's customs and traditions. When visiting holy places, greet people with a handshake or a kiss on both cheeks, dress modestly, and be respectful of local sensibilities.

Try the local food: the Costa Brava is famous for its delectable Catalan cuisine. Try traditional meals such as paella, fideuà, and botifarra to immerse yourself in the region's gastronomic pleasures. To experience the tastes of the Mediterranean, visit local markets and eateries.

Do go beyond the coast: While coastal towns and beaches are beautiful, don't confine yourself to them. In the interior, you'll find picturesque towns, wineries, and natural parks. Explore the countryside to get a full picture of Costa Brava.

Do engage in responsible tourism: Responsible tourism demonstrates respect for the environment. Avoid trash, hike on approved routes, and avoid hurting or destroying any flora or animals. Only footprints are left, and only memories are taken.

While credit cards are generally accepted, it's always a good idea to have extra cash on hand, particularly for smaller shops and markets that may not take cards. Make sure you have enough cash on hand for little purchases, tips, and emergencies.

Use sunscreen: Costa Brava has a Mediterranean climate, and the sun may be harsh, especially in the summer. Apply sunscreen with a high SPF, wear a hat, and wear sunglasses to protect your skin and eyes.

Do visit the local markets: The Costa Brava has active local markets where you may immerse yourself in the local culture. To experience fresh fruit, local delicacies, and artisan crafts, go to markets like the Mercat de Sant Josep in Barcelona or the Mercat Municipal in Girona.

While many people understand English, learning a few simple words in Catalan or Spanish may go a long way toward demonstrating respect and admiration for the local language and culture. Simple greetings and emotions are appreciated.

Don'ts:

Don't forget to verify your train or bus tickets: It's essential to confirm your tickets before entering public transit, particularly trains and buses. Failure to do so may result in fines or penalties if ticket inspectors catch you.

Keep an eye on your possessions and avoid leaving them unattended: As with any trip location, it's critical to keep an eye on your goods and avoid leaving them unattended. To avoid theft or loss, keep an eye on your personal possessions, particularly in popular tourist locations.

Don't litter: Because Costa Brava is proud of its natural beauty, it's crucial to preserve the environment by avoiding littering. Put your rubbish in designated containers or carry it with you until you reach an appropriate disposal location. Contribute to keeping Costa Brava clean and lovely for everybody to enjoy.

Don't disregard beach safety instructions: When visiting Costa Brava's beaches, pay heed to the safety guidelines issued by lifeguards. Swim in approved locations, obey warning signs, and be wary of underwater currents. Your safety should always come first.

Respect religious places: When visiting religious sites in Costa Brava, like as churches or cathedrals, dress modestly and behave responsibly. Remember that these locations have cultural and spiritual importance for the local community.

Don't depend only on credit cards: While credit cards are generally accepted, carrying cash is usually a smart idea. Cash may be the sole acceptable method of payment in tiny towns or local enterprises.

Tips for Finding Low-Cost Accommodation in Costa Brava

If you want to save money on your Costa Brava hotel, there are numerous ways you may use to uncover low-cost solutions. Here are some pointers to help you find low-cost lodging:

Plan and Book Early: Booking your accommodations early may typically result in better bargains and cheaper pricing. Begin researching and reserving your accommodations as soon as you have your vacation dates confirmed in order to take advantage of early bird discounts and availability.

Travel During Off-Peak Seasons: The summer months are peak tourist seasons in Costa Brava, and costs tend to be higher. Consider going during the shoulder or off-season seasons, when costs are lower. Not only will you discover lower prices, but you will also find fewer crowded attractions and a more relaxing atmosphere.

Be Flexible with Dates and destinations: Being flexible with your trip dates and destinations will provide you with additional possibilities for inexpensive lodging. Consider rearranging your vacation dates or visiting alternative places along the Costa Brava coast. Rates may vary greatly based on the time of year and location.

Use Comparison Websites: Use hotel and lodging comparison websites to compare rates from various suppliers. Websites like as Booking.com, Hotels.com, and Expedia enable you to compare prices, read reviews, and get the best offers for the dates and places you choose.

Consider different Accommodation Types: Look beyond standard hotels for different lodging possibilities. Guesthouses, bed & breakfast facilities, hostels, and vacation rentals are often less expensive than luxury hotels. These alternatives may offer pleasant and cost-effective lodging.

Stay in Smaller Towns or Villages Outside of main Tourist destinations: Consider staying in smaller towns or villages outside of main tourist destinations. Rates are often cheaper, yet you'll still have convenient access to Costa Brava's attractions and beaches. Even if you are not staying in a central area, public transit makes it easy to explore the region.

Sign up for hotel loyalty programs to get access to member-only discounts, special deals, and benefits. With each booking, you'll earn points that may be used for future stays or upgrades. If you often go to Costa Brava or other places, loyalty programs may bring long-term advantages.

Consider Self-Catering Options: If you choose lodgings with kitchens, such as flats or vacation rentals, you may save money on eating out. You may save money by preparing your own meals utilizing local items from markets and supermarkets.

Look for Package bargains: Look for bargains that bundle lodging, airfare, and activities. Bundled packages are often offered by travel companies and internet platforms, and they may result in considerable savings when compared to buying each component individually.

Read Reviews and Ratings: When searching for low-cost lodging, be sure to read reviews and ratings from prior visitors. This will allow you to assess the accommodation's quality and dependability, ensuring that you're receiving excellent value for your money.

By following these suggestions, you may increase your chances of obtaining affordable lodging in Costa Brava without sacrificing comfort or quality. Remember to shop around, be flexible, and prepare ahead of time to get the greatest bargains for your stay.

CHAPTER 2: Making Travel Plans to Costa Brava.

A vacation to Costa Brava needs meticulous planning and preparation to guarantee a pleasant and pleasurable experience.

Here are some crucial measures to help you efficiently organize your trip:

Determine Your Stay Duration: Determine how long you plan to stay in Costa Brava. Consider how many days you have available for your trip and how much time you want to spend on different activities and sites.

Choose the Best Time to Visit: When deciding when to visit Costa Brava, consider the temperature and tourism seasons. Summer months (June to August) are the busiest for tourists, as are the beaches. Spring and fall provide lovely weather and less tourists.

Make your itinerary: Research and select the sights and attractions in Costa Brava that you want to see. To obtain a full picture of the area, include a mix of coastal towns, cultural landmarks, natural parks, and local markets.

Set a Budget: Determine your trip budget, including hotels, transportation, food, activities, and any other costs. Consider the cost of flights or transportation to Costa Brava, the sort of lodging you choose, and the activities you intend to participate in.

Book a Room: Look for appropriate lodging that fits your budget and preferences. Costa Brava has a variety of accommodations, including hotels, resorts, guesthouses, and vacation rentals. Book your lodgings ahead of time, particularly during high season, to ensure the finest selection.

Investigate Transportation Options: Investigate the various modes of transportation available in Costa Brava. Choose if you want to hire a vehicle, use public transit, or do both. Based on your itinerary, consider the ease, affordability, and accessibility of various means of transportation.

Plan Your Activities: Determine the activities and sights you want to see in Costa Brava. This might entail going to the magnificent beaches, seeing cultural places like as the Dal Theatre-Museum or the Girona Cathedral, trekking along coastal paths, or delighting in local food. Make a list of must-see sights and schedule your days accordingly.

Check Visa Requirements: Make sure you have the proper visas or travel papers to enter Spain and, if applicable, the Schengen Area. Check the visa requirements for your home country and apply ahead of time if required.

Pack Appropriately: When preparing for your vacation, keep the weather and activities in mind. Pack seasonally suitable attire, such as swimsuits, comfortable walking shoes, sunscreen, hats, and sunglasses. Don't forget to bring travel adapters, chargers, and any required prescriptions.

While English is commonly understood in tourist regions, learning a few simple words in Catalan or Spanish may improve your interactions with people and demonstrate respect for the local culture. Simple greetings and courteous remarks may make a big difference.

Purchase Travel Insurance: Travel insurance that covers medical emergencies, trip cancellation, and lost or stolen possessions is highly advised. Investigate several insurance companies and choose a coverage that meets your requirements.

Check Health and Safety standards: Before heading to Costa Brava, review the most recent health and safety standards and cautions. Keep up to date on any travel restrictions, vaccine needs, or particular advice relating to the continuing worldwide epidemic.

Make a Travel Checklist: Create a list of necessary things and chores to perform before your trip. This may involve passports, tickets, travel insurance documentation, currency conversion, and advising your bank of your vacation intentions.

Inform Family and Friends: Inform your family and friends about your vacation intentions, including your itinerary and contact information. It's usually a good idea to have someone know where you are in case of an emergency.

Insurance for Travel

When planning a vacation to Costa Brava or any other place, it is essential to think about getting travel insurance. Travel insurance gives financial security and peace of mind in the event of an unforeseen occurrence or emergency while on vacation. Here are some important facts concerning travel insurance:

Coverage

Medical expenditures: Medical expenditures are often covered by travel insurance, including emergency medical care, hospital stays, and, if required, medical evacuation.

Vacation Cancellation or Interruption: If your vacation is canceled or interrupted due to unexpected circumstances like sickness, accident, or a family emergency, travel insurance may compensate you for non-refundable charges including flights, hotels, and activities.

Travel insurance may provide coverage for lost, stolen, or delayed baggage, allowing you to recover the value of your goods or compensate you for critical items while you wait for your luggage.

Travel Delays: If your journey is delayed due to factors beyond of your control, such as bad weather or airline strikes, travel insurance may cover extra expenditures, such as lodging and food.

Personal Liability: Personal liability coverage may be included in travel insurance if you cause property damage or harm someone by accident while on vacation.

Travel Insurance Types

Single journey Insurance: This sort of insurance covers a single journey and is appropriate for infrequent travelers.

Yearly/Multi-Trip Insurance: If you travel often, a yearly or multi-trip insurance may provide cost-effective coverage by covering numerous journeys within a set time range.

Some insurers provide group insurance that cover numerous people traveling together, such as families or tour groups.

Selecting the Best Policy:

Assess Your Needs: To calculate the coverage you need, consider your travel plans, the duration of your vacation, the activities you'll be doing, and the worth of your goods.

Read the Policy Details: Carefully examine the policy language, coverage limitations, exclusions, and terms and conditions to verify they match your unique requirements. Take note of any pre-existing medical problems that may have an impact on coverage.

Compare quotations: Request quotations from several insurers and compare coverage, features, and prices to determine which insurance provides the greatest value for your money.

Examine Existing Insurance Policies: Examine your existing insurance policies, such as health insurance or credit card coverage, to see what coverage you already have and if extra travel insurance is required.

Purchasing Travel Insurance

Get Early: It is suggested that you get travel insurance as soon as you plan your trip in order to cover any unforeseen occurrences that may arise prior to your departure.

Investigate Reputed Insurers: Select a reputed insurance carrier with a proven track record of processing claims and delivering excellent customer service.

Understand the Claims procedure: Become familiar with the claims procedure and associated documents so you know what to do if you need to file a claim during your trip.

Travel insurance is an important investment that may protect you from financial losses and help you in times of need. Consider your travel plans, evaluate your requirements, and choose the appropriate coverage to ensure a worry-free vacation to Costa Brava and any future travel excursions.

Travel Documents and Visa Requirements.

It is essential to be informed of the visa requirements and appropriate travel papers before arranging a trip to Costa Brava. Consider the following crucial points:

Costa Brava is situated in Spain, which is a member of the Schengen Area. If you are not a citizen of a country exempt from the Schengen visa requirement, you will need to get a Schengen visa in order to visit Costa Brava. The Schengen visa permits you to stay in the Schengen Area for up to 90 days during a 180-day period.

Exemptions: Certain nations' citizens do not need a visa to visit the Schengen Area for tourist reasons. The United States, Canada, Australia, New Zealand, Japan, and several European nations are among them. However, since exemptions differ by country, it is important to examine the precise visa requirements for your nationality.

Valid Passport: Whether or whether you need a visa, you must have a valid passport to access Costa Brava. Check that your passport is valid for at least six months beyond your scheduled departure date from the Schengen Area.

Visa Application Process: If you need a Schengen visa, you must apply at your home country's Spanish consulate or embassy. Typically, the application procedure is filling out an application form, supplying supporting documentation (such as evidence of lodging, airplane bookings, travel insurance, and financial means), and paying the visa price.

Timeline for Application: It is best to apply for your Schengen visa well in advance of your anticipated trip dates. The processing time varies based on the consulate or embassy and the season. Check the consulate's website for detailed information on processing timelines and any other requirements.

Travel Insurance: Obtaining a Schengen visa requires the purchase of travel insurance. Check that your travel insurance policy covers medical emergencies, repatriation, and a minimum of €30,000 in coverage. The insurance should be valid during your stay in the Schengen Area.

Supporting Papers: You will need to supply numerous supporting papers while applying for a Schengen visa. Flight tickets, hotel bookings or evidence of lodging, a detailed itinerary, proof of financial means (such as bank statements), a trip insurance policy, and a completed visa application form are examples of acceptable documentation.

Border Control: When you arrive in Costa Brava, you will travel through border control to have your passport and visa (if required) verified. Ensure that all required documentation are readily accessible for examination.

If you want to remain in Costa Brava for more than 90 days or participate in activities like as job, education, or long-term residence, you must apply for a visa or permission before visiting. Because these visas have various criteria and application procedures, it is important to do your homework and apply correctly.

Check the most recent information on visa requirements and travel paperwork for Costa Brava according on your nationality. For thorough and precise information on your individual situation, contact the closest Spanish consulate or embassy or visit their official websites.

How to Get to Costa Brava.

Costa Brava is a lovely seaside location in northeastern Spain. Depending on your starting place, there are numerous methods to get to this breathtaking site. To help you plan your travel, below are some typical modes of transportation:

By Air:

Girona-Costa Brava Airport (GRO): Girona Airport is the nearest airport to Costa Brava, located around 30 kilometers away. It is an important entry point for visitors to the region. Many low-cost airlines fly to Girona Airport from cities around Europe.

Barcelona-El Prat Airport (BCN): Another handy alternative is Barcelona's international airport, which is situated around 100 kilometers south of Costa Brava. You may easily reach Costa Brava by rail, bus, or rental vehicle from the airport.

Taking the Train

High-Speed Trains: Spain's AVE high-speed rail network links major cities such as Barcelona and Madrid to Girona. From there, you may take regional trains or buses to several towns along the Costa Brava coast.

Renfe runs regional rail services that link Girona to coastal communities like as Blanes, Lloret de Mar, and Tossa de Mar. These trains provide a lovely travel along the coast and are a handy way to explore the area.

By Bus

Bus Services: Several bus companies provide frequent services from major Spanish cities, notably Barcelona, to several communities on the Costa Brava. Popular bus companies that provide links to coastal sites include ALSA and Sagalés. The bus ride enables you to take in the region's scenic sights.

By Car

Rental vehicle: Renting a vehicle allows you to explore Costa Brava at your own leisure. Major vehicle rental businesses have locations at airports and towns around Spain. The AP-7 highway travels next to the shoreline, linking numerous municipalities along the Costa Brava.

Driving from Barcelona: From Barcelona, use the C-32 or AP-7 highways towards Girona and continue down the coast to your selected Costa Brava resort.

Ferry writes

Ferry from France: If you are traveling from France, you may take a ferry from Nice, Marseille, or Toulon to Barcelona or adjacent ports. You may continue your trip to Costa Brava by rail, bus, or rental vehicle from there.

Consider variables such as cost, convenience, and travel time while arranging your vacation to Costa Brava. It's best to reserve your transit tickets or hire a vehicle ahead of time, particularly during high travel seasons. Remember to double-check the most recent schedules and availability to guarantee a pleasant and pleasurable trip to this lovely area of Spain.

7 Days Itinerary for Costa Brava Visitation

Day 1: Arrival and exploration in Barcelona

- Arrive in Barcelona and check into your hotel.
- Spend the day visiting the bustling metropolis. Admire Antoni Gaud's architectural marvels in the landmark Sagrada Familia and Park Güell.
- Take a leisurely walk along La Rambla, immersing yourself in the vibrant environment and eating local delights from the food vendors.

Excursion to Girona and Figueres on Day 2

- Visit Girona, a lovely city noted for its well-preserved medieval architecture, for a day excursion. Explore Girona Cathedral and meander through the Jewish Quarter's small alleyways.
- In the afternoon, go to Figueres to see the Dal Theatre-Museum, a surrealist masterpiece devoted to Salvador Dal's works.
- Return to Barcelona in the evening for a leisurely meal at a nearby restaurant.

Tossa de Mar and Coastal Exploration on Day 3

- Visit the lovely seaside village of Tossa de Mar. Take in panoramic views of the Mediterranean Sea from the old Tossa de Mar Castle.
- Spend the day relaxing on Platja Gran, the main beach, or participating in water sports like as snorkeling or paddleboarding.
- Savor the fresh tastes of the area with a delicious seafood supper at a seaside restaurant.

Day 4: Cadaqués and Salvador Dal Visit

- Cadaqués, a lovely beach community noted for its white-washed buildings and bohemian ambiance, is a must-see.
- Visit the Salvador Dal House-Museum near Portlligat Bay, the artist's old home. Explore the exhibit to learn more about Dal and his creative vision.
- Take a lovely stroll along the beach walkways and take in the Mediterranean scenery.
- Return to your lodging and unwind for the evening.

Day 5: Natural Park of Cap de Creus and Outdoor Adventure

- Visit Cap de Creus Natural Park, a rocky and wild coastline region, for a day excursion.
- Hike the nature paths and marvel at the breathtaking cliffs, secluded coves, and panoramic overlooks.
- Explore the Cap de Creus Lighthouse, positioned on the Iberian Peninsula's easternmost point.
- Explore the marine life of the area by participating in water sports such as kayaking or snorkeling.
- Return to your lodging and have a well-earned rest.

Day 6: Relaxation and Beaches

- Spend the day relaxing on the Costa Brava's lovely beaches. Visit lesser-known beaches like as Aigua Blava, Sa Tuna, and Cala Pola.
- Enjoy the sun, swim in the pristine seas, and relax on the sandy beaches.
- Enjoy beachside eating while enjoying the coastal vistas, tasting local delicacies and cool beverages.
- Take a leisurely evening walk down the seaside promenade and soak in the serene atmosphere.

Day 7: Exploration of Barcelona and Departure

- Return to Barcelona for the last day of your Costa Brava vacation.
- Visit any remaining Barcelona sights or sites that you may have missed on the first day.
- Explore the bustling areas of Barri Gtic and El Born for unique boutiques, local markets, and fashionable cafés.
- Travel back to Barcelona with wonderful recollections of your Costa Brava experience.

This 7-day trip combines the dynamic metropolis of Barcelona with cultural excursions to Girona and Figueres, seaside exploration in Tossa de Mar and Cadaqués, and outdoor experiences in Cap de Creus Natural Park. It enables a perfect

Currency and Banking in Costa Brava

The Euro (€) is the official currency of Spain, including the Costa Brava area. Although cash is advised for modest transactions, credit and debit cards are generally accepted in most businesses, including hotels, restaurants, and stores. ATMs are widely available across the Costa Brava, enabling you to withdraw cash in Euros using your debit or credit card.

Banking: Here are some important facts regarding banking in Costa Brava:

Banks & Hours of Operation:

Banks in Costa Brava are normally open Monday through Friday, with some branches shutting for a siesta in the afternoon. The precise hours of operation may vary, however most banks are open from 8:30 a.m. to 2:00 p.m., with some bigger branches being open until 5:00 p.m.

It's worth noting that banks are closed on weekends and holidays. ATMs, on the other hand, are open 24 hours a day, seven days a week.

ATMs:

ATMs are extensively accessible in towns, cities, and prominent tourist sites along the Costa Brava. You may use your debit or credit card to withdraw cash in Euros.

To enhance security and prevent possible skimming devices, utilize ATMs situated inside banks or recognized organizations.

Inform your bank or credit card issuer of your trip intentions to prevent having your cards stopped due to suspicious behaviour.

Credit and Debit Cards are Accepted.

In Costa Brava, credit and debit cards, notably Visa and Mastercard, are frequently accepted. They are suitable for the majority of transactions, including hotel payments, restaurant bills, and shopping. Carrying numerous cards from various providers as a backup is always a smart idea in case one card is lost, stolen, or malfunctions.

Extra locations may have a minimum purchase requirement for card payments, so having extra cash on hand for minor transactions is beneficial.

Currency Conversion

Banks, currency exchange offices, and some bigger hotels provide currency exchange services. To obtain the greatest value for your money, compare exchange rates and fees.

Avoid converting cash at airports or tourist locations since the rates and taxes are generally less beneficial.

Travelers' Checks:

Traveler's checks are less frequent nowadays, and many places may refuse to take them. It is encouraged that you use debit and credit cards, as well as cash, for your transactions.

Safety Recommendations

When using ATMs or making card payments, stay aware of your surroundings and protect your PIN to avoid theft or fraud.

To reduce the danger of pickpocketing, keep your cards and cash in a safe location, such as a money belt or a concealed pocket.

It's crucial to note that this information is based on general practices, and you should always verify with your bank and credit card issuer for particular specifics on fees, use, and foreign travel alerts. You can guarantee a pleasant and comfortable financial experience during your vacation by being prepared with the correct money and knowing the banking choices in Costa Brava.

Areas to Avoid in Costa Brava

While Costa Brava is typically a secure and lovely place, there are a few spots that some visitors may want to avoid while selecting lodging. Here are some things to keep in mind:

Lively Party Zones: Certain neighborhoods, especially in bigger cities like as Lloret de Mar, are renowned for their bustling nightlife and party culture. While these places may be appealing to tourists looking for a vibrant environment, they may be loud and congested, particularly during the high summer season. If you want a more calm and relaxing atmosphere, it is best to stay away from the major party zones.

Too Touristy Spots: Some spots along the Costa Brava coast, particularly during the summer months, may become too touristy. While these neighborhoods may have a variety of services and activities, they may also be busy and pricey. Consider staying in smaller towns or villages that are less touristy if you want a more genuine and less crowded experience.

Remote and Isolated Locations: While the rural regions and solitary sites on the Costa Brava provide solitude and magnificent natural beauty, they may not be suited for all vacationers. Facilities, food choices, and transit links may be restricted in remote regions. Choose lodgings near towns or cities along the coast if you desire quick access to services and activities.

High Crime Areas: In general, the Costa Brava is considered safe for visitors. However, as with any major tourist location, occasional cases of petty theft or pickpocketing may occur. It's best to be cautious, particularly in congested places and tourist sites. Keep an eye on your surroundings, safeguard your belongings, and adhere to basic safety procedures.

When choosing a place to stay, investigate the region and read reviews from past visitors to get a sense of the ambience and compatibility for your needs. It's also a good idea to talk to locals or ask for advice on travel forums to get the most up-to-date information on particular locations to avoid.

Overall, Costa Brava has a broad variety of attractive and secure places to stay, so with careful study and preparation, you may locate the ideal accommodation to enjoy your vacation to this magnificent part of Spain.

Getting Around on the Costa Brava

Once you've arrived at Costa Brava, travelling about the area is simple. Here are some popular types of transportation for exploring the region:

By Bus:

Bus Services: The most prevalent means of transportation for visitors in Costa Brava is public buses. Several local bus companies operate along the coast, connecting cities and villages. Sarfa, Sagalés, and Teisa are popular operators. Tickets may be purchased on board, in advance at bus terminals, or online.

Taking the train

Regional Trains: Renfe has regional trains that link coastal communities such as Blanes, Lloret de Mar, and Tossa de Mar. The railway is a great way to go to more isolated spots along the coast. Tickets may be purchased at railway stations or online.

By Car

Rental vehicle: If you want to explore the area at your own leisure, renting a vehicle is a great alternative. The majority of major automobile rental firms, including Girona-Costa Brava Airport, have branches in Costa Brava. The AP-7 highway travels along to the ocean, linking villages along its length. However, be prepared for some tight and twisty roads.

By Bicycle

Cycling: The Costa Brava is a popular cycling destination owing to its gorgeous routes and diverse topography. Most villages along the coast provide bike rentals or guided riding trips. The region includes designated bike lanes, and several routes provide breathtaking views of the beach.

On Foot:

Walking is an excellent way to discover the natural beauty of Costa Brava. The Camino de Ronda, which travels along the coast, is one of numerous hiking pathways. You may also walk around the old towns and villages.

Traveling by Boat

Boat Tours: Exploring the shoreline and adjacent islands by boat is a popular activity. There are various alternatives available, including catamarans, sailing boats, and glass-bottom boats. The majority of boat cruises leave from large coastal cities and villages such as Blanes, Lloret de Mar, and Tossa de Mar.

Consider cost, convenience, and the length of your route while arranging your transportation. Check the most recent schedules and availability, particularly during high travel seasons. Costa Brava, with its different landscapes and attractions, provides an amazing experience, and there are several ways to explore the area.

Communication and Language in Costa Brava.

Catalan is the major language spoken in Costa Brava, as well as the rest of Catalonia and Spain. However, since Costa Brava is a major tourist destination, many people in the area also speak Spanish (Castilian) and English. Here are some key aspects to understand regarding language and communication in Costa Brava:

Catalan is a language spoken in Catalonia.

The official language of Catalonia, which encompasses Costa Brava, is Catalan. It is widely spoken by the locals and is utilized in government papers, signs, and public services.

You may come across street signs, eateries, and informative items printed in Catalan when visiting Costa Brava. Locals will appreciate your knowledge of a few simple Catalan words, which will improve your cultural experience.

Castilian (Spanish):

Spanish, sometimes known as Castilian, is widely understood and spoken across the Costa Brava. Many residents, notably those in the tourist business, speak Spanish well.

If you speak Spanish, speaking with people and traversing Costa Brava will be pretty simple. Even if you don't know Spanish, many individuals in the area can grasp simple English phrases.

English

English is widely spoken in Costa Brava's tourist districts, hotels, restaurants, and significant attractions. Staff at these places often speak English and may provide you with information and services.

It is crucial to remember, however, that English competence varies among people, particularly in more rural locations or smaller companies. To enhance conversation, it is usually beneficial to acquire a few fundamental words in Catalan or Spanish.

Language Pointers

Learn simple Phrases: Learn some simple Catalan or Spanish phrases for greeting people, asking for directions, ordering meals, and expressing appreciation. Locals will appreciate your attempt to learn a few native terms.

Use Translation Apps: If you face language obstacles, use translation apps or bring a phrasebook with you. These tools may assist you in overcoming language barriers and ensuring easier communication.

Cultural Awareness

Respect Catalan customs and traditions to embrace the local language and culture. Using simple words and demonstrating an interest in learning the local language may lead to pleasant encounters with the people.

While English is commonly understood in many tourist places, making an effort to learn a few basic Catalan or Spanish words may improve your trip experience and establish links with the local population. The inhabitants of Costa Brava value tourists who are interested in their language and culture, and even a few basic phrases may go a long way toward developing memorable conversations during your stay.

Health and Safety in Costa Brava.

When visiting Costa Brava, it is important to prioritize your health and safety in order to have a pleasant and pleasurable experience. Here are some important health and safety considerations:

Travel Protection

Purchase comprehensive travel insurance that includes coverage for medical expenditures, trip cancellation or interruption, and emergency medical evacuation. Ascertain that your insurance policy offers appropriate coverage for your particular requirements and activities in Costa Brava.

Medical Services

Costa Brava boasts modern medical services such as hospitals, clinics, and pharmacies. Seek aid from these institutions if you have any medical emergency or healthcare demands.

Carrying a basic first aid pack with vital drugs and supplies for minor accidents or illnesses is recommended.

Vaccinations

Consult your healthcare physician or a travel medicine expert before heading to Costa Brava to ensure you are up to date on standard vaccinations and to enquire about any specialized vaccines suggested for the location.

Vaccinations for hepatitis A, hepatitis B, typhoid, and tetanus may be suggested depending on your travel plans and personal health.

Protection against the sun

Costa Brava has a Mediterranean climate with plenty of sunlight, especially in the summer. Wear sunscreen with a high SPF, sunglasses, and a hat to protect yourself from damaging UV radiation. To avoid sunburn and heatstroke, seek shelter during high sun hours.

Food Safety and Hygiene

Maintain appropriate hygiene habits, such as washing your hands with soap and water on a frequent basis, particularly before eating or handling food. Consume food that is safe and hygienically prepared. Select trustworthy restaurants and organizations, and be certain that the meat and fish are adequately cooked. To avoid drinking tap water, use bottled water or use a water filtration system.

Precautions for Safety

- Use standard safety measures such as being alert of your surroundings, safeguarding your possessions, and storing valuables in hotel safes.
- Swim with caution in the sea, since certain spots may have strong currents or hazardous ground. Pay attention to caution signals and obey the instructions of lifeguards.
- Follow safety requirements, utilize suitable equipment, and be aware of possible dangers while participating in outdoor activities such as hiking or water sports.

Emergency Phone Numbers

Learn the emergency phone numbers in Costa Brava, including those for medical crises (ambulance), police, and fire services. In Spain, the universal emergency number is 112.

It's always a good idea to remain updated on your destination's health and safety recommendations and cautions. Check your government's travel advisories or official tourist websites for the most up-to-date information on health, safety, and travel restrictions in Costa Brava.

You may have a wonderful and worry-free vacation to Costa Brava by taking the required measures and being conscious of your health and safety.

Customs and Etiquette in Costa Brava

When visiting Costa Brava, it is both courteous and entertaining to get acquainted with the local traditions and etiquette. Here are some crucial items to remember:

Politeness and greetings: When meeting someone, it is usual to shake hands and establish eye contact. Friends or acquaintances may share a kiss on both cheeks in more informal circumstances.

When addressing someone you don't know well, it's courteous to use formal titles (Sr. for males and Sra./Srta for women) until they welcome you to use their personal name.

When speaking with locals, always say "por favor" (please) and "gracias" (thank you), whether at a restaurant, store, or anywhere else.

Respect and personal Space

Personal space is valued in Spanish and Catalan cultures, and physical contact is often more restricted than in other cultures. Respect the personal space of people and avoid needless physical contact until requested to do so.

It is important to be aware of noise levels, particularly in residential areas, hotels, and public transit. Keep talks and music at a moderate level, especially late at night and early in the morning.

Dining Protocol:

It is traditional at restaurants to wait to be seated rather than picking a table oneself.

When dining with locals, it is customary to wait for the host or the oldest person to begin eating before beginning your meal.

Try local foods and specialties, and be open to new culinary experiences. Tapas or tiny dishes are often shared among a group.

Remember that a tip is normally included in the bill, but it's always nice to offer a tiny extra tip for great service.

Formal Attire is Required.

Costa Brava offers a calm and easygoing attitude, especially around the shore. In most instances, casual attire is fine.

It is appropriate to dress modestly and avoid wearing exposing or beach clothes while visiting religious locations or more formal events.

Pack good walking shoes since Costa Brava has magnificent vistas and exploring options.

Siesta Hours

Siesta is a customary afternoon break enjoyed in several Spanish locales, including the Costa Brava. Some stores, offices, and services may shut or have reduced hours during siesta time, which is normally between 2:00 PM and 5:00 PM.

It is best to schedule your activities properly, and keep in mind that certain places may be closed during this period.7

Language

While many Costa Brava residents understand English, making an effort to acquire a few basic Catalan or Spanish words might be beneficial. Locals often welcome tourists who attempt to speak in their language, even if it is only a hello or thank you.

Celebrations & Festivals

The Costa Brava is well-known for its lively festivals and festivities. If you chance to be in the neighborhood during a local festival, take advantage of the opportunity to observe and join in the activities. Respect local customs and adhere to any event guidelines or restrictions.

You may enrich your cultural experience and demonstrate appreciation for the local way of life by being aware of and following local traditions and etiquette. The inhabitants of Costa Brava are typically kind and would appreciate your attempts to learn about and accept their traditions.

Here are some useful phrases and words to help you communicate during your visit to Costa Brava:

Greetings and Basic Phrases

Hola - Hello

Buenos días - Good morning

Buenas tardes - Good afternoon

Buenas noches - Good evening/night

Adiós - Goodbye

Por favor - Please

Gracias - Thank you

De nada - You're welcome

¿Cómo estás? - How are you?

Mucho gusto - Nice to meet you

Disculpe - Excuse me

Directions and Transportation

¿Dónde está...? - Where is...?

¿Cómo llego a...? - How do I get to...?

Estoy perdido/a - I'm lost

¿Cuánto cuesta? - How much does it cost?

Autobús - Bus

Tren - Train

Taxi - Taxi

Aeropuerto - Airport

Estación de tren - Train station

Parada de autobús - Bus stop

Izquierda - Left

Derecha - Right

Recto - Straight ahead

Arriba - Up

Abajo – Down

Food and Dining

Carta/menú - Menu

Quisiera... - I would like...

¿Qué recomiendas? - What do you recommend?

Una mesa para dos, por favor - A table for two, please

¿Tienes...? - Do you have...?

Agua - Water

Vino - Wine

Cerveza - Beer

Pan - Bread

Carne - Meat

Pescado - Fish

Postre – Dessert

Shopping

¿Cuánto cuesta? - How much does it cost?

¿Tienes esto en otro color/talla? - Do you have this in another color/size?

Quiero comprar esto - I want to buy this

¿Aceptas tarjetas de crédito? - Do you accept credit cards?

Rebajas - Sales

Tienda - Shop/store

Mercado - Market

Euros – Euros

Emergencies

Ayuda - Help

Necesito un médico - I need a doctor

Llame a la policía - Call the police

Estoy perdido/a - I'm lost

¡Cuidado! - Be careful!

Fuego - Fire

Remember, even attempting a few basic phrases in the local language can go a long way in showing respect and making connections with the locals. The people of Costa Brava will appreciate your effort to communicate in their language, and it can enhance your overall travel experience.

Costa Brava Accommodation Options

Costa Brava has a variety of lodging alternatives to accommodate a variety of interests, budgets, and travel types. Whether you choose luxury, comfort, or a more affordable stay, the area has sufficient possibilities. Here are some popular Costa Brava lodging options:

Hotels: Costa Brava offers a wide range of accommodations, from magnificent resorts to boutique hotels and budget-friendly alternatives. There are beachfront hotels with spectacular sea views, centrally positioned hotels in attractive cities, and hidden rural retreats to pick from. Major cities such as Lloret de Mar, Tossa de Mar, and Roses have a diverse range of hotels to suit a variety of budgets and interests.

Resorts: Costa Brava is home to a number of resorts that provide a full experience with amenities such as pools, spa facilities, restaurants, and entertainment choices. These resorts often provide visitors immediate beach access as well as programmed activities. They are an excellent solution for individuals looking for leisure and ease while on vacation.

Guesthouses and Bed & Breakfasts: Consider staying in a guesthouse or bed and breakfast for a more private and customized experience. These establishments are often family-run and provide comfortable rooms with a homey environment. The kind hosts will serve you a great breakfast and provide you with insider information.

Holiday Rentals: Apartments, villas, and cottages are available for rent on the Costa Brava. This option is perfect for families or big parties since it offers more room and the freedom to prepare your own meals. Holiday rentals are accessible in a variety of locales, including coastal districts and scenic rural settings.

Camping: Costa Brava includes various campsites and caravan parks for those who prefer camping. These campgrounds cater to tents, caravans, and RVs and are often located near the beach or in natural preserves. Camping is an excellent opportunity to see the natural beauty of the area while also participating in outdoor activities.

Agrotourism: Costa Brava also has agrotourism possibilities, including rural farmhouses and agritourism resorts. These lodgings enable you to explore the countryside and participate in activities like farming, wine tours, and horseback riding. It's a one-of-a-kind approach to engage with environment and local culture.

Consider variables such as location, facilities, closeness to activities, and your budget when choosing your lodging. To ensure your preferred option, book ahead of time, particularly during high travel seasons. Booking.com, Airbnb, and TripAdvisor can give a complete list of available rooms in Costa Brava, as well as reviews and ratings from past visitors.

Luxury, Mid-Range, and Budget-Friendly Accommodation options In Costa Brava.

Costa Brava has a variety of lodgings to accommodate a variety of budgets and interests. Here are several significant alternatives in the premium, mid-range, and budget-friendly pricing ranges, as well as their locations:

Luxury Hotels:

Hotel Camiral at PGA Catalunya Resort: This luxury resort in Caldes de Malavella provides large accommodations, a spa, golf courses, and great dining choices. Prices start at about €250 per night.

Mas de Torrent Hotel & Spa: This five-star hotel in Torrent has exquisite rooms, a spa, an outdoor pool, and a Michelin-starred restaurant. Prices per night vary from €350 to €800.

Hotels in the Mid-Range:

Hotel Santa Marta: This four-star hotel in Lloret de Mar offers pleasant accommodations, direct beach access, a swimming pool, and a restaurant. Prices begin about €100 per night.

Hotel Aigua Blava: This quaint hotel in Begur provides pleasant rooms with sea views, an outdoor pool, a restaurant, and easy access to local beaches. The nightly rate ranges from €120 to €200.

Budget-Friendly Accommodations

Hostel Sa Rascassa: Located in Calella de Palafrugell, this budget-friendly hostel has dormitory-style and private rooms, as well as a shared kitchen and a patio. Prices start at about €30 per night.

Hostal Empries: This budget-friendly alternative in L'Escala offers modest but pleasant accommodations, an on-site restaurant, and a beachside position. The nightly rate ranges from €60 to €100.

Mas Patoxas Camping Resort-Bungalow Park: Located in Pals, this camping resort provides a variety of cheap lodgings, including bungalows and mobile homes. Prices begin at €40 per night.

Prices may vary based on the season, availability, and accommodation type. For the most current and up-to-date price information, contact each accommodation directly or via booking sites. Consider variables such as location, amenities, and closeness to attractions while selecting hotels. Luxury resorts give great facilities and services for a luxurious experience, whilst mid-range hotels provide pleasant accommodations with extra conveniences. Budget-friendly solutions, such as hostels and camping resorts, provide more economical options without sacrificing basic conveniences.

Remember to book ahead of time, particularly during high travel seasons, to ensure that you get the best pricing on your favorite accommodations. Costa Brava boasts a variety of hotels to fit any traveler's preferences and budget, whether you're looking for luxury, mid-range, or budget-friendly alternatives.

Here are some pointers for a stress-free travel to Costa Brava:

Arrange ahead of time: Conduct research and arrange your schedule, including accommodations, transportation, and activities. This will allow you to make the most of your time and prevent stress at the last minute.

Make a list of everything you'll need for your vacation, including clothes, toiletries, and any devices or chargers. Pack little, particularly if you want to travel around a lot.

Prepare for the weather: Before traveling to Costa Brava, check the weather forecast and pack appropriately. Summers may be hot and dry, while winters can be chilly and wet.

While many people in Costa Brava understand English, knowing some basic Spanish phrases will help you converse with locals and make your vacation more pleasurable.

Respect local traditions and etiquette: To avoid upsetting locals and to better immerse oneself in the culture, learn about local customs and etiquette, such as clothing regulations and dining etiquette.

Keep your valuables secure: Avoid carrying large quantities of money or wearing costly jewelry in busy places. To keep your valuables safe, use a money belt or carry a lockable bag.

Keep hydrated: Because the Mediterranean environment in Costa Brava may be hot and dry, it's important to keep hydrated. Carry a water bottle with you at all times and drink lots of water.

Use public transportation: The Costa Brava has an excellent network of buses and trains that are both inexpensive and convenient. To save money and avoid traffic, consider using public transit instead of renting a vehicle.

Try the local cuisine: Costa Brava is well-known for its delectable seafood and regional cuisine. Take advantage of the chance to eat local delicacies and learn about the local culinary scene.

Be open to new experiences: Costa Brava is a varied and lively area with a rich history and culture. Keep an open mind and be ready to try new things, whether it's new meals or new hobbies.

Packing Essentials

When preparing for your vacation to Costa Brava, it's crucial to travel light and just bring the essentials. Consider the following packing essentials:

Clothing:

Pack lightweight and breathable clothes appropriate for the Mediterranean environment, such as shorts, t-shirts, dresses, and skirts.

Swimwear: Costa Brava offers great beaches, so bring your swimwear.

Light layers: For chilly nights or air-conditioned settings, bring a light jacket or sweater.

Pack suitable walking shoes or sandals since Costa Brava provides many options for exploration.

Wear a wide-brimmed hat and sunglasses to protect yourself from the sun.

Rain jacket or travel umbrella: Because rain showers might occur on occasion in Costa Brava, it's a good idea to bring a compact rain jacket or travel umbrella.

Documents for Travel

Passport: Make sure your passport is valid for at least six months beyond the date of travel.

Visa: Determine if you need a visa to visit Costa Brava depending on your country and the length of your stay.

Carry a copy of your travel insurance policy and emergency contact numbers with you.

Itinerary and lodging information: Maintain a hardcopy or electronic copy of your itinerary, including hotel bookings and contact information.

Accessories and electronics

The Costa Brava employs Europlug (Type C) electrical outlets, therefore pack a universal adaptor if necessary.

Mobile phone and charger: Keep your phone charged and close at hand.

Camera: Use a camera or smartphone to capture the stunning scenery and vistas of Costa Brava.

Items for Personal Care

Bring travel-sized items such as toothbrushes, toothpaste, shampoo, conditioner, and sunscreen.

Drugs: If you need prescription drugs, make sure you bring enough for the length of your vacation.

Pack a basic first-aid kit containing band-aids, pain remedies, antiseptic cream, and any personal prescriptions.

Money and Necessities:

Local currency: Bring some euros with you for little purchases and establishments that may not take credit cards.

Credit/Debit Cards: Bring at least one major credit card and notify your bank of your vacation intentions to prevent card difficulties.

A travel wallet or pouch will keep your vital papers, money, and cards organized and protected.

To secure your baggage, use a tiny combination or key lock.

Comfort and Entertainment:

Books or E-reader: If you prefer reading, bring a book or e-reader with you for downtime leisure.

Travel pillow and blanket: A travel cushion and blanket may enhance comfort to lengthy flights or road journeys.

Earphones or headphones: Block out noise or listen to music or podcasts while traveling.

Remember to verify your airline's or transportation provider's luggage limitations and weight limits to avoid any unnecessary expenses. Pack just what you really need to make your baggage manageable and allow space for any keepsakes you may wish to bring home.

Tips for Local Transportation in Costa Brava

Because of its well-connected transportation infrastructure, getting about Costa Brava is pretty simple. Here are some pointers to assist you navigate local public transportation:

Buses: The Costa Brava has a well-developed bus network that links major cities and tourist attractions. The bus service is dependable, reasonably priced, and provides picturesque trips. For timetables and rates, contact the local bus operator, such as Sarfa or Moventis. Tickets may be purchased at bus terminals or straight from the driver upon boarding.

Trains: Another handy mode of transportation throughout Costa Brava is the train. The regional railroad network links communities along the coast, offering a convenient and efficient mode of transit. Rodalies de Catalunya is the regional railway company. Check the timetables and rates before of time, and think about buying tickets at the station or online.

Taxis: Taxis may be hailed on the street or obtained at authorized taxi stands on the Costa Brava. Before beginning the trip, be sure the taxi has a functional meter or negotiate a rate. Taxis are a good choice for short excursions or when traveling with bags.

Renting a vehicle might be a wonderful alternative if you desire more freedom and independence. The roads in Costa Brava are well-maintained, and owning a vehicle enables you to visit off-the-beaten-path sites. There are many vehicle rental businesses in the area, so it's better to book ahead of time and check costs to get the best offers.

Cycling: The Costa Brava has wonderful coastline paths and stunning surroundings that are ideal for cyclists. Bicycle rentals are available in many cities and rental businesses, enabling you to explore at your own leisure. Look for designated bike trails or ask tourist information centers for suggested routes.

Strolling: Because the seaside towns on the Costa Brava are frequently tiny and pedestrian-friendly, strolling is a pleasant and convenient way to get about. Walking enables you to immerse yourself in the local culture, uncover hidden treasures, and quickly reach stores, restaurants, and attractions.

Ferries: Consider taking a ferry if you want to see adjacent islands or coastal towns. Ferry services to destinations like the Medes Islands and Cadaqués are available from coastal communities like Blanes and Roses. Check the timetables and rates before of time since they may change depending on the season.

Plan ahead of time by familiarizing yourself with transit timetables and routes. Examine the operation hours, frequency of service, and any special rules or restrictions. Planning ahead of time will allow you to maximize your time and minimize surprises or delays.

Verify Tickets: Before boarding buses or trains, be sure to verify your tickets if you're using public transit. Look for ticket validation machines at stations or on buses, and then follow the instructions. Fines may be imposed if tickets are not validated.

Consider utilizing travel applications or websites to have access to real-time timetables, maps, and route planning tools. Apps like Moovit and Google Maps may assist you in smoothly navigating the local transit system.

You can make the most of your stay in Costa Brava by familiarizing yourself with the local transportation choices and arranging your itineraries ahead of time.

Costa Brava Safety Precautions

While Costa Brava is typically a secure place for vacationers, some care must be taken to guarantee a safe and pleasurable experience. Here are some precautions to take:

Keep an eye on your surrounds: Keep an eye on your surroundings, particularly in busy locations, tourist sites, and public transit. Keep an eye on your possessions and avoid overtly exhibiting precious stuff.

Use a money belt or a lockable bag to protect your valuables, such as passports, wallets, and devices, from pickpockets. Avoid leaving your items unattended for even a second.

Stay in well-lit and populous locations: Especially at night, stick to well-lit streets and populated neighborhoods. Avoid wandering alone in unfamiliar or desolate regions, especially in remote portions of cities or on beaches.

Choose Dependable Transportation: When traveling, choose licensed taxis or reputed transportation providers. Use unlabeled or unauthorized vehicles at all costs. If feasible, plan ahead of time for transportation via trusted firms.

Swimming safety precautions include paying attention to warning flags and following lifeguard directions while swimming in the water. Swim in approved places and be aware of strong currents. Consider using a life jacket if you are not a good swimmer.

Respect the Natural Environment: Costa Brava is endowed with stunning natural landscapes, which must be respected and preserved. When hiking, camping, or visiting natural areas, follow the requirements and leave no litter behind.

Remain hydrated and sun-protected: The Mediterranean sun may be harsh, so drink lots of water to remain hydrated. Wear sunscreen, a hat, and seek shade during the warmest hours of the day.

Follow Local Laws and Traditions: Get to know the local laws and customs so you can remain on the right side of the law and respect the local culture. Be aware of any restrictions on photography, clothing standards, or conduct at religious places.

Carry Identification: Always have a copy of your passport or another form of legitimate identification with you. Place the original document in a secure location, such as a hotel safe.

Save Emergency Contact Numbers, such as local police, ambulance, and your embassy or consulate, on your phone or write them down. Knowing who to call in an emergency may be really useful.

Consider getting travel insurance that covers medical emergencies, trip cancellations, and lost or stolen possessions before your trip. Examine the policy specifics and have a duplicate of the insurance information handy.

Trust your instincts: If anything or someone seems strange or hazardous, trust your instincts and exit the situation. It is preferable to be cautious and prioritize your own safety.

You may have a worry-free and joyful trip visiting the gorgeous Costa Brava area if you follow these safety tips. Remember that being prepared and aware of your surroundings is critical to having a safe and enjoyable journey.

Costa Brava Etiquette & Environmental Respect.

It is essential to respect local customs, traditions, and environmental preservation while visiting Costa Brava. Here are some etiquette suggestions and techniques to demonstrate environmental sensitivity:

Greetings & Politeness: It is usual to greet individuals in Costa Brava with a handshake and a warm "Hola" (hello) or "Buenos das/tardes/noches" (good morning/afternoon/evening). When communicating with locals, restaurant workers, or service providers, use "por favor" (please) and "gracias" (thank you).

While Costa Brava is renowned for its laid-back beach vibe, it's still vital to dress correctly, particularly when visiting religious sites or upmarket places. When entering churches or other religious places, cover your shoulders and knees.

While many Costa Brava residents understand English, it is welcomed when tourists learn a few basic Spanish words. Simple greetings and phrases such as "Cómo estás?" (How are you?) "Por favor" (Please), and "Gracias" (Thank you) may go a long way toward expressing respect and connecting with the locals.

Respect for Cultural Sites: Be mindful of the laws and restrictions while visiting historical or cultural sites such as castles, museums, or monuments. To conserve the sites for future visitors, follow any rules about photographing, touching artifacts, or designated walkways.

Environmental Awareness: The Costa Brava has great natural beauty, and it is essential to respect and safeguard the environment. Follow these rules for responsible tourism:

Hike on approved trails and walkways to prevent hurting vulnerable habitats. Properly dispose of rubbish and recycle wherever feasible. Keep a small bag for garbage collection until you discover a proper disposal container.

Conserve water and energy by being conscious of your hotel and lodging consumption.

Encourage environmentally friendly and sustainable enterprises that focus environmental practices.

In natural regions, avoid plucking flowers or upsetting animals.

Do not leave rubbish on the beach or in the water. Remove your rubbish and leave the beach clean.

Noise and Public Behavior: Be courteous of other visitors and residents by keeping noise levels low, particularly in residential areas or late at night. Avoid disruptive activity that might upset the tranquility or local communities.

Tipping is not required in Costa Brava, but is appreciated for good service. If you are pleased with the service, a 5-10% gratuity is customarily left in restaurants. Before tipping, check to see whether a service fee has already been included to the bill.

Local items and Crafts: Buy locally created items and crafts to support the local economy. This helps to preserve traditional craftsmanship while also benefiting the local community.

You may contribute to a happy and peaceful tourist experience in Costa Brava while protecting its natural and cultural legacy for future generations by following these etiquette recommendations and demonstrating respect for the environment.

Sagrada Familia.

The Sagrada Familia is an iconic basilica and Barcelona's most recognized monument. This magnificent masterpiece, designed by famous architect Antoni Gaud, mixes Gothic and Art Nouveau styles. The ornate façade, towering spires, and spectacular stained glass windows of the basilica make it a must-see destination. Visitors are met by an enthralling environment rich with natural light and unique furnishings. The continuous building of the Sagrada Familia is a tribute to Gaud's vision, and seeing the work in progress is a once-in-a-lifetime opportunity.

Park Güell

Park Güell is a UNESCO World Heritage Site and a wonderful public park designed by Antoni Gaud. With brilliant mosaic-covered buildings, twisting walkways, and quirky sculptures, the park exemplifies Gaud's particular aesthetic. Visitors may stroll around the park's gardens, take in panoramic views of Barcelona, and see Gaud's home, which has been converted into a museum. Park Güell is not only a tribute to Gaud's artistic talent, but it also provides a peaceful escape in the middle of nature.

La Rambla

One of Barcelona's most renowned avenues, La Rambla is a lively tree-lined promenade. It spans from Plaça de Catalunya to the waterfront and has a lively ambiance as well as a variety of stores, cafés, and street entertainers. Visitors may view the colorful flower shops, wander through the local markets, and visit sights such as Barcelona's famed opera theatre, the Gran Teatre del Liceu. Despite its popularity, La Rambla maintains its allure and functions as a bustling hive of activity.

Girona

Girona church, commonly known as the Cathedral of Saint Mary of Girona, is a spectacular Gothic church situated in the centre of the city. It is a sight to see, with its massive exterior, beautiful brickwork, and majestic nave. Visitors may climb the cathedral's stairs to get a bird's-eye view over the city, or they can tour the interior, which has a large collection of religious art and relics. The cathedral's beauty and historical importance make it a must-see in Girona.

The Jewish Quarter (Call Jueu)

Girona's Jewish Quarter is a charming district recognized for its well-preserved medieval streets and historical importance. It is one of Europe's best-preserved Jewish neighborhoods and provides insight into the city's Jewish legacy. Visitors may view the Museum of Jewish History and sites such as the Bonastruc ça Porta Centre while strolling through small cobblestone alleys. The Jewish Quarter has a wonderful ambience, with quaint lanes, secret courtyards, and a feeling of antiquity at every step.

Girona City Walls

Girona's city walls are a tribute to the city's rich history and provide an interesting approach to learn about it. Walking around the city walls offers breathtaking views of the city, including the magnificent Old Town and surrounding countryside. The walls date back to the Roman era, although they have been enlarged and reinforced throughout time. The experience of wandering along the walls provides a feeling of adventure as well as an opportunity to observe Girona's architectural grandeur from a new viewpoint.

Figueres.

Theatre-Museum: Figueres is recognized for being the birthplace of Salvador Dal, one of the twentieth century's most acclaimed painters. The Dal Theatre-Museum was created by Dal himself and is a surrealistic masterpiece. The museum is home to large collection of Dal's works, which include paintings, sculptures, and installations. With its unique design and unexpected architectural components, the building itself is a piece of art. Inside, guests may explore the numerous galleries and exhibition rooms and immerse themselves in Dal's bizarre universe. The museum provides a unique glimpse into the thoughts of this amazing artist and is a must-see for art lovers and Dal fans alike.

Tossa de Mar

Tossa de Mar Castle: A medieval fortification dating back to the 12th century, Tossa de Mar Castle is perched on a hill overlooking the sea. The castle's strong stone walls, turrets, and battlements form a stunning setting against the Mediterranean's blue waves. The inside of the castle, which includes a small museum displaying relics from Tossa de Mar's past, is open to visitors. Views of the sea and the picturesque town below may be viewed from the castle walls. The castle represents Tossa de Mar's rich legacy and provides a look into the town's medieval past.

Platja Gran (Main Beach): Tossa de Mar has numerous magnificent beaches, with Platja Gran, often known as the Main Beach, being the most popular. It is the ideal place to relax and soak up the sun, with its golden beach, crystal-clear seas, and gorgeous location. The beach has many of facilities, such as sun loungers, umbrellas, and beachside eateries. Visitors may participate in a variety of aquatic sports, such as swimming, snorkeling, or just strolling along the promenade. The panoramic splendor of Platja Gran, as well as its enticing seas, make it a must-see destination for beachgoers.

Cadaqués

Salvador Dal House-Museum: Cadaqués is a lovely seaside village where Salvador Dal found inspiration. For many years, the Salvador Dal House-Museum in Portlligat served as the artist's house and workplace. The home itself is a one-of-a-kind construct that reflects Dal's quirkiness and creative vision. Visitors may tour the house's different rooms, which are packed with personal items, artwork, and oddities. The museum gives insight into Dal's life and creative process, providing a fascinating view into the realm of one of history's greatest surrealists.

Portlligat Bay: Portlligat Bay is a beautiful cove in Cadaqués recognized for its quiet environment and breathtaking natural beauty. The harbor is flanked by rugged cliffs and is studded with colorful fishing boats, making for a picturesque backdrop. Visitors may unwind on the pebbled beach, swim in the pristine waters, or just enjoy the peace and quiet. The attractiveness and natural nature of the bay make it a hidden treasure on the Costa Brava.

Natural Park of Cap de Creus

Cap de Creus Lighthouse: Located at the easternmost point of the Iberian Peninsula, the Cap de Creus Lighthouse is a light that stands majestically on the rough coastline of the Cap de Creus Natural Park. The lighthouse provides amazing panoramic views of the sea and shoreline. Hiking routes lead to the lighthouse, where visitors may marvel at the spectacular natural sceneries along the way. Cap de Creus' rocky cliffs, secret bays, and raw beauty make it a nature lover's and outdoor enthusiast's heaven.

Hiking and Nature routes: Cap de Creus Natural Park is a paradise for outdoor lovers, with a variety of hiking and nature routes to explore. From easy beach walks to strenuous alpine hikes explorations; the park offers something for everyone. The routes travel through a variety of environments, such as steep cliffs, lush woods, and meandering seaside roads. Hikers may explore secret beaches, enjoy panoramic views, and meet rare flora and animals along the route. The park also has numerous well-marked trails, including the GR 92 long-distance track, which provides a multi-day hiking excursion. Exploring the hiking and nature paths of Cap de Creus Natural Park is a memorable experience, whether you're a seasoned hiker or a casual nature enthusiast.

The best Costa Brava attractions provide an enthralling combination of cultural, artistic, and natural treasures. Each place has its own distinct allure, from the architectural wonders of Barcelona to the ancient charm of Girona and the strange world of Salvador Dal in Figueres and Cadaqués. Costa Brava delivers a varied and rewarding experience for every tourist, whether you're touring ancient places, resting on magnificent beaches, or immersing yourself in nature. So pack your luggage, go off on an adventure, and let the charm of Costa Brava unfold before you.

Beaches and Coastal Recreation

Costa Brava is well-known for its beautiful beaches and scenic coastline. The area provides a wealth of possibilities for beach lovers and water enthusiasts, with its crystal-clear seas, golden dunes, and craggy cliffs. Here's a comprehensive list of the beaches and coastal activities that help to make Costa Brava a genuine paradise:

Aro's Platja:

Platja d'Aro is a well-known coastal town famed for its lovely sandy beaches and lively atmosphere. Platja Gran, the major beach, runs for approximately 2 kilometers and provides plenty of room for sunbathing and enjoyment. Kayaking, paddleboarding, and jet skiing are among the water sports available. The promenade is dotted with stores, restaurants, and bars, which creates a vibrant atmosphere both during the day and at night.

Palafrugell de Calella

Calella de Palafrugell is a delightful fishing resort with beautiful coves and beaches. El Golfet, a little hidden bay surrounded by cliffs and crystal-clear seas, is one of the most renowned beaches. Cala del Canadell and Port Pelegr are two more prominent beaches in the vicinity. Visitors may swim, snorkel, or just relax and enjoy the calm beauty of these hidden jewels.

Tuna Sa Tuna:

Sa Tuna is a charming fishing community tucked away in a rocky inlet. The beach is modest yet attractive, with brilliant blue seas and a laid-back ambiance. It's an excellent location for sunbathing, swimming, and snorkeling. The hamlet itself has a few restaurants that provide great seafood meals, enabling guests to appreciate the local delicacies while taking in the surroundings.

Aiguablava:

Aiguablava is well-known for its breathtaking natural beauty and clear seas. The beach is bordered by pine trees and steep cliffs, providing a peaceful and scenic atmosphere. The pure blue waters are ideal for swimming and snorkeling, enabling tourists to explore the vibrant underwater environment. Aiguablava also rents boats, enabling you to explore the coast and find secret coves and isolated beaches.

Roses:

Roses is a bustling seaside town with a kilometer-long sandy beach. Beachfront bars, water sports facilities, and volleyball courts are among the attractions available at the beach. It's a great area for family-friendly activities, with beach games, sunbathing, and leisurely stroll down the beach. Visitors may also take boat journeys from Roses to see the magnificent Cap de Creus Natural Park and its rocky coastline scenery.

Hiking and walking along the coast:

Aside from its gorgeous beaches, Costa Brava has a plethora of coastal walks and hiking paths that enable tourists to immerse themselves in the region's natural splendor. The Cam de Ronda is a well-known coastal walk that runs along the coast and provides access to secret coves and isolated beaches. The trail travels past cliffs, pine trees, and picturesque coastal towns, making for a memorable hike.

Scuba Diver:

Costa Brava is a scuba diving destination for people looking for underwater activities. Numerous diving sites with various marine habitats, such as underwater caves, rocky reefs, and colourful marine life, may be found in the area. Medes Islands, where you can see colorful fish and even octopuses, and the Cap de Creus Marine Reserve, recognized for its great biodiversity, are also popular diving locations.

Excursions via boat:

Boating around the Costa Brava coastline is an excellent opportunity to explore secret coves, isolated beaches, and stunning cliffs. There are a variety of boat excursions offered, ranging from peaceful sightseeing tours to thrilling speedboat rides. Some trips even give you the chance to

Sports on the water

Costa Brava is a water sports enthusiast's paradise, with a diverse choice of exhilarating activities for all ability levels. Whether you want adrenaline-pumping thrills or a relaxing day on the sea, the area provides something for everyone. Here are some of the most popular water sports in Costa Brava:

Surfing

The Costa Brava coastline is well-known for its excellent surf conditions, which draw surfers from all over the world. Platja Sant Pol in Sant Feliu de Guxols and Playa de Pals in Begur are well-known for their regular waves, making them great surfing destinations. Whether you're a novice or a seasoned surfer, there are surf schools and rental businesses along the coast that provide equipment and training.

SUP (Stand-Up Paddleboarding):

Stand-up paddleboarding has grown in popularity in recent years, and the calm seas of Costa Brava make it an ideal location for this pastime. SUP lets you to explore the coastline at your own speed while taking in the scenery and getting a wonderful exercise. Paddleboards may be rented at several coastal rental businesses, or you can join guided trips to explore secret coves and gorgeous beaches.

Kayaking:

Kayaking around the Costa Brava coastline is an excellent opportunity to find secret coves, explore sea caves, and take in the breathtaking scenery. Kayaks may be rented from many beaches, or you can join organized trips that include equipment and expert guides. Kayaking enables you to get up close and personal with the region's rocky cliffs, abundant marine life, and quiet beaches that are otherwise unreachable by foot.

Jet skis:

Jet skiing is a popular option for an intense water adventure. Several Costa Brava coastal villages and resorts have jet ski rentals, enabling you to speed through the waves and enjoy a thrilling trip. You may hire jet skis for a specific period of time and explore the coast at high speed, whether you're a novice or an experienced rider.

Parasailing:

Parasailing is a thrilling and one-of-a-kind sport that enables you to fly far above the beach while taking in panoramic views of the sea and surrounding scenery. You'll be safely tethered to a parachute and dragged by a speedboat while you experience the sensation of flight. Professional instructors assure your safety during the activity, which is accessible in a variety of coastal cities and beach resorts.

Windsurfing:

The good wind conditions on the Costa Brava make it an ideal place for windsurfing. The high winds and waves provide a perfect setting for both novice and experienced windsurfers. Windsurfing centers and rental facilities may be found at beaches such as Sant Pere Pescador and Sant Marti d'Empuries. You may learn to scuba dive, rent equipment, and experience the sensation of gliding through the sea.

Kiteboarding:

Kiteboarding is a thrilling water activity that combines aspects of surfing, windsurfing, and wakeboarding. With its consistent winds and wide beaches, the Costa Brava coastline is ideal for kiteboarding. If you're new to kiteboarding, there are schools that provide instruction as well as equipment rental. Kiteboarders with prior experience may enjoy the freedom of surfing the waves and doing stunning aerial tricks.

Scuba Diver:

Underwater exploration is a must-do activity in Costa Brava. Diverse marine environments, vivid coral reefs, and intriguing marine life may be found in the area. There are various dive facilities along the coast that provide guided dives, equipment rental, and diving training, whether you are a licensed diver or a novice. Discover the hidden gems under the surface and immerse yourself in the aquatic beauty of Costa Brava.

Fishing:

Fishing in Costa Brava is a great option for people looking for a more calm sea sport.

Mountain biking and hiking.

Hiking and mountain biking are popular outdoor sports in Costa Brava because of the varied scenery and well-maintained paths. Whether you prefer a relaxing stroll along beach roads or a difficult mountain bike ride across mountainous terrain, Costa Brava has something for everyone. Here's a rundown of hiking and mountain biking opportunities in the area:

Hiking

Cam de Ronda: The Cam de Ronda is a well-known coastal route that runs the length of the Costa Brava. It takes you past lovely coastal villages, secret bays, and steep cliffs while offering stunning views of the Mediterranean Sea. The track is well-marked and suited for hikers of all fitness levels, with possibilities for short parts or multi-day walks.

Cap de Creus Natural Park: The Cap de Creus Natural Park is a hiker's paradise, with a network of paths winding through its breathtaking vistas. You may discover the park's rocky coastline, craggy mountains, and distinctive flora and animals on pleasant walks or demanding climbs. The highlight is reaching the Cap de

Creus Lighthouse, from where you can enjoy panoramic views of the Mediterranean.

Montgr Massif: The Montgr Massif is a mountain range in the vicinity of Estartit. It has a variety of hiking paths for people of all experience levels. The most popular trek is to Montgr Castle, which offers panoramic views of the surrounding region. The massif is also home to a variety of species and provides an opportunity to discover its natural splendor.

Garrotxa Volcanic Zone Natural Park: The Garrotxa Volcanic Zone Natural Park is a wonderful trekking destination located inland from Costa Brava. There are dormant volcanoes, lush forests, and volcanic landscapes in the park. Several well-marked routes travel through the park's natural treasures, including the famed Fageda d'en Jordà, a beech forest growing on a volcanic lava plain.

Cycling in the mountains

Les Gavarres is a mountain range located between Girona and the seashore. It has a large network of routes for mountain bikers of all skill levels. There's something for everyone, from easy rides through the woods to more difficult technical courses. The routes lead you through beautiful scenery such as lush woods, rolling hills, and lovely towns.

Collserola Natural Park: While not exactly on the Costa Brava, Collserola Natural Park is readily accessible from Barcelona and has good mountain riding options. The park has a variety of paths for people of all ability levels, including cross-country and downhill riding. While cycling around the park, you may take in spectacular views of the city and surrounding countryside.

La Garrotxa's volcanic landscapes not only give excellent hiking options, but also exhilarating mountain biking paths. Mountain cyclists looking for a challenge will love the tough terrain, natural parks, and hilly vistas. The paths vary in difficulty and length, enabling riders to explore the area's volcanic topography and lush woodlands.

Vall de Ribes: Vall de Ribes is a hilly location in the Pyrenees that provides amazing mountain bike adventures. The region has a network of paths of varied difficulties that enable cyclists to experience the Pyrenean landscapes, which include woods, rivers, and mountain summits. The breathtaking scenery and adrenaline rush of downhill descents make it a popular destination for mountain bikers.

It is important to be prepared and follow safety precautions before beginning on any hiking or mountain bike activity. Always bring water, wear suitable footwear and gear, and keep track of trail and weather conditions.

Golfing

Golfing in Costa Brava is a wonderful experience for those who like this sophisticated activity. The area is home to a number of golf courses that include stunning scenery, tough fairways, and first-rate amenities. Costa Brava, with its nice temperature and beautiful surroundings, is the ideal setting for a wonderful golfing trip. The following are some prominent golf courses in the area:

Catalunya PGA Resort:

The PGA Catalunya Resort, located near Girona, is widely regarded as one of Europe's top golf complexes. The Stadium Course and the Tour Course are both championship courses. The Stadium Course has hosted a number of international events and is well-known for its difficult layout and natural splendor. The Tour Course is more forgiving while still delivering a challenging golf experience. There are also superb practice facilities, a golf school, and a clubhouse with exquisite eating choices within the property.

Empordà Country Club

The Empordà Golf Club in Gualta has two 18-hole courses: Links and Forest. The Links course has undulating fairways, pot bunkers, and coastal vegetation for a typical links-style play. The Forest course, nestled among pine trees and lakes, has a more parkland-like layout. Both courses provide unique challenges, breathtaking vistas, and a fantastic golfing experience. A driving range, practice grounds, and a clubhouse with a restaurant and pro shop are all available at the club.

Platja de Pals Golf

Golf Platja de Pals is one of the Costa Brava's oldest golf courses, located near the town of Pals. This 18-hole course mixes parkland and links aspects to create a one-of-a-kind golfing experience. The course is placed in a stunning natural setting of pine trees, dunes, and lakes. It provides a reasonable challenge for golfers of all ability levels. A pro shop, practice facilities, and a restaurant with panoramic views of the course are available at the club.

Aro Golf Club

Golf d'Aro is a lovely course nestled in the hills of Platja d'Aro that provides spectacular views of the Mediterranean Sea. The undulating fairways, strategic bunkers, and high tees distinguish this 18-hole course. It provides a fun challenge for golfers of all skill levels. The clubhouse has a café and balcony, as well as practice facilities and a golf school.

Costa Brava Golf Club

Club de Golf Costa Brava is a well-established golf course in a peaceful setting near Santa Cristina d'Aro. The 18-hole course has parkland and forest characteristics, as well as tight fairways and strategic water hazards. The layout provides a reasonable challenge while rewarding precision and clever play. There are practice grounds, a pro shop, and a clubhouse with a restaurant and bar at the club.

When organizing a golf vacation to Costa Brava, it is best to verify availability and book reservations ahead of time. Many golf courses provide packages that include lodging, golf rounds, and other amenities. It's also worth remembering that certain courses have clothing requirements and need handicap certificates. Costa Brava's golf courses provide a wonderful golfing experience in a magnificent Mediterranean environment, whether you're a seasoned player or a novice.

Ballooning by Hot Air.

Hot air ballooning in Costa Brava is an intriguing and fascinating experience that enables you to fly above the region's breathtaking scenery. It provides panoramic views of the magnificent coastline, rolling hills, attractive towns, and lush farmland from a unique vantage point. Hot air ballooning is a must-do activity in Costa Brava if you're looking for an exciting experience as well as a peaceful vacation. What you need to know about hot air ballooning in the area is as follows:

Locations for Ballooning

Several firms provide hot air balloon trips in Costa Brava, with launch points situated across the region. Areas surrounding Girona, Empordà, and the Pyrenees foothills are popular launch places.

Each site has its own distinct landscape and character, offering a great experience no matter where you fly.

Time of flight

A normal Costa Brava hot air balloon ride lasts around an hour, depending on weather and wind patterns. However, the whole experience, including preparations, balloon inflation, and landing, may take three to four hours. Balloon rides are often held early in the morning or late in the afternoon, when the weather conditions are ideal for a safe and pleasurable flight.

Views of Nature

As you soar into the skies, you'll be treated to stunning vistas of the Costa Brava area. The gorgeous Mediterranean coastline, with its golden beaches, turquoise waves, and towering cliffs, may be seen from above. The charming towns, vineyards, olive groves, and sweeping countryside are revealed in the rural settings. On clear days, you could even see the Pyrenees Mountains in the distance.

Relaxing Experience

As the balloon floats smoothly in the air, hot air ballooning provides a tranquil and pleasant experience. Unlike other modes of aircraft, there is no noise or engine, letting you to enjoy the peace and beauty of the surroundings. It's an ideal chance to unwind, reconnect with nature, and get away from the hurry and bustle of daily life.

Pilots with prior experience

Costa Brava hot air balloon flights are operated by professional and trained pilots who emphasize safety and assure a smooth and pleasurable journey. They are well-versed in the region's weather patterns and provide useful comments along the drive. You may relax knowing that you are in the hands of specialists who put your safety and comfort first.

Considerations for the Weather

Weather is a factor in hot air ballooning, and flights are contingent to good weather conditions. Weather predictions and wind patterns are meticulously monitored by balloon operators to assess the viability of each voyage. If the weather does not cooperate, the flight may be postponed at a later day. It is critical to preserve flexibility and have backup plans in case of weather-related disruptions.

Sizes of Groups

Hot air balloon baskets may accommodate a variety of party sizes, from intimate two-person rides to larger group events. Some companies provide private flights for couples or small groups, while others may handle parties of 10 or more. Consider your choices and choose the one that best meets your requirements.

Safety Precautions:

While hot air ballooning is typically safe, it is critical to follow the pilot and crew's directions. You will be given a safety briefing before boarding the balloon, which will contain crucial information regarding the flight and landing procedures. It's critical to pay attention, ask questions, and follow the pilot's instructions throughout the encounter.

Hot air ballooning in Costa Brava is an unforgettable excursion that enables you to admire the region's natural beauty from a completely different perspective. To guarantee your space, book your hot air balloon flight in advance, particularly during busy tourist seasons. Prepare your camera to capture the breathtaking scenery.

Catalan Traditional Dishes

Catalan cuisine is noted for its rich flavors, fresh ingredients, and unusual sweet and salty flavor combinations. Catalan foods, influenced by Mediterranean, Spanish, and French culinary traditions, highlight the region's dynamic gastronomy. Here are some classic Catalan foods to try on your trip to Costa Brava:

Pa amb Tomàquet: This classic Catalan cuisine consists of bread rubbed with ripe tomatoes, drizzled with olive oil, and seasoned with salt. It's frequently served as a complement to other dishes or savored on its own. A wonderful explosion of tastes is created by the combination of crusty bread, juicy tomatoes, and high-quality olive oil.

Escalivada: Escalivada is a grilled vegetable dish made with roasted eggplant, bell peppers, and onions. To generate a smokey taste, the veggies are scorched over an open flame before being peeled and sliced. They are often seasoned with olive oil, garlic, and vinegar. Escalivada is often served as a tapa or side dish, and its deep, earthy flavor is popular among locals.

Botifarra amb Mongetes: Botifarra sausages, grilled or roasted, are served with white beans in this typical Catalan meal. Botifarra sausages are produced with pork, spices, and herbs, and have a meaty and flavorful taste. The sausages are often fried until crispy on the surface, while the soft white beans serve as a creamy and filling side dish.

Fideuà: Fideuà is a famous Catalan seafood meal similar to paella, except instead of rice, it utilizes fideus, which are short, thin noodles. The noodles are boiled in a savory broth with shrimp, squid, and mussels, and are seasoned with garlic, tomatoes, and spices. Traditionally, the meal is prepared in a broad, shallow pan known as a "paella" and served with aioli sauce on the side.

Crema Catalana: A creamy custard with a caramelized sugar topping, Crema Catalana is a traditional Catalan dessert. The custard is made with egg yolks, milk, sugar, and a dash of citrus zest and is boiled until thickened before being refrigerated. The sugar topping is caramelized using a blowtorch or under a broiler just before serving, producing a wonderful contrast between the creamy custard and the crunchy caramelized coating.

Canelons: Canelons, also known as Catalan cannelloni, are a popular meal eaten on special occasions or on Sundays. They are made out of spaghetti tubes filled with a combination of ground meat, such as beef and pig, and sometimes leftover roasted meat from prior meals. The packed pasta is then baked in a thick béchamel sauce and topped with grated cheese, yielding a warm and savory meal.

Xató: A classic Catalan salad composed of endive, salted codfish, anchovies, olives, and romesco sauce. The romesco sauce contains roasted tomatoes, red peppers, almonds, hazelnuts, garlic, and bread crumbs. The acidic romesco sauce, which adds depth of flavor and compliments the other components, is frequently drizzled over the salad.

Suquet de Peix: Suquet de Peix is a hearty fish stew that originated in Catalonia's coastal districts. It usually consists of a variety of local fish and shellfish, such as monkfish, prawns, clams, and mussels, cooked in a delicious broth of tomatoes, garlic, onions, white wine, and olive oil. The stew is sometimes served with crusty bread to mop up the flavorful soup.

These are only a few examples.

Use local Restaurants and Grocery Stores.

When visiting Costa Brava, you will be able to sample the region's diverse gastronomic scene by visiting local restaurants and food markets. Whether you like traditional Catalan cuisine or cosmopolitan cuisines, Costa Brava provides a diverse choice of eating alternatives to suit your tastes. Here are some prominent local eateries and food markets to check out:

El Celler de Can Roca (Girona): Located in Girona, El Celler de Can Roca is a world-renowned restaurant. It boasts three Michelin stars and has constantly been regarded as one of the top restaurants in the world. The Roca brothers make recipes that highlight local ingredients and Catalan characteristics. Their tasting menu takes you on a culinary experience that mixes creativity, precision, and delectable tastes.

Compartir (Cadaqués): Compartir is a prominent restaurant in Cadaqués' charming center. The restaurant was founded by three former El Bulli chefs and has a cuisine centered on shared dishes. The recipes are influenced by Catalan and Mediterranean tastes, and they include fresh seafood, local ingredients, and inventive presentation. The comfortable and inviting ambiance enhances the eating experience.

Sa Xarxa (Tossa de Mar): Sa Xarxa is a delightful seafood restaurant in Tossa de Mar. It serves traditional Catalan cuisine, with a focus on fresh seafood dishes. Sa Xarxa provides a delectable mix of tastes that highlight the region's seaside wealth, from grilled sardines and paella to seafood stew and pickled anchovies.

Can Roca (Roses): Can Roca is a family-run restaurant located in Roses. It has a long history of offering great traditional Catalan food. The menu emphasizes meals crafted with fresh, locally sourced ingredients that accentuate regional tastes. The restaurant's welcoming atmosphere and excellent service provide a great dining experience.

Mercat de la Boqueria (Barcelona): Mercat de la Boqueria, located in the center of Barcelona, is one of the city's most renowned food markets. It has a lively and busy ambiance, with merchants offering a wide range of fresh fruit, meats, fish, cheeses, spices, and other items. It's a terrific location to learn about the local culinary culture, try traditional Catalan dishes, and buy items to make your own meals.

Mercat de Sant Josep de la Boqueria (Girona): Mercat de Sant Josep de la Boqueria is Girona's equivalent of Mercat de la Boqueria. This vibrant market features the finest of the region's food, including fruits, vegetables, cured meats, cheeses, and regional delicacies. It's an excellent location for exploring the brilliant colors, scents, and sensations of the local cuisine scene.

Plaça de l'Abat Oliba (Figueres): Plaça de l'Abat Oliba in Figueres has a weekly food market with a broad range of fresh local vegetables, baked delicacies, regional wines, and more. The market provides a genuine experience in which you can connect with local sellers, sample their goods, and learn about the regional cuisines.

These are just a handful of the many outstanding restaurants and food markets in Costa Brava. Exploring these culinary places will provide you with a better understanding of the region's gastronomic past and enable you to sample the different tastes of Costa Brava's native cuisine.

Wine and Cava Tasting

Costa Brava is well-known for its high-quality wines and sparkling cavas. Several wineries and vineyards in the area provide wine and cava tastings, allowing tourists to learn about the local wine culture. Here are some wine and cava tasting advice for Costa Brava:

Empordà Wine area: The Empordà wine area is located on the Costa Brava and produces a range of high-quality wines. The peculiar tastes of the wines are affected by the region's unique terroir, which is influenced by the Mediterranean Sea and the Pyrenees Mountains. Consider visiting wineries in Empordà, such as Masia Serra, Castillo de Perelada, or Mas Llunes, to get a personal look at local wine production.

Wine Tasting Tours: A wine tasting tour is a great opportunity to learn about the wines of Costa Brava. These trips usually include visits to many vineyards, where you may taste a variety of wines and learn about the winemaking process. Tours are often given by qualified experts who provide information about the region's winemaking traditions, grape types, and tasting procedures.

Cava Production: Costa Brava is also well-known for the production of cava, a typical sparkling wine. Cava is primarily made in the Penedès area, which is close to the Costa Brava. Consider taking a day trip to Penedès to visit cava producers such as Freixenet, Codornu, or Gramona, where you can learn about the process and sample cava.

Wine and Food matching: Wine and food go hand in hand, and Costa Brava provides the ideal setting for wine and food matching experiences. Wine matching menus are available at many vineyards and local restaurants, with wines carefully picked to suit the tastes of each meal. This enables you to enjoy the balance between the wines and the gastronomic pleasures of the area.

Wine Festivals: Throughout the year, Costa Brava conducts a number of wine festivals to celebrate the local wine culture. These festivities are colorful and celebratory, with tastings, music, and typical Catalan food. The Cadaqués Wine Festival and the Girona Wine Festival are two prominent wine festivals in the area.

Wine Shop Visits: If you want a more autonomous wine tasting experience, you may visit Costa Brava's wine shops and cellars. These places often provide a large range of local wines and cavas, enabling you to sample and pick your favorite bottles. The employees at wine stores may provide suggestions and explain the various wines offered.

Wine and Cava Museums: Costa Brava also has numerous wine and cava museums where you can learn about the region's wines' history, production processes, and cultural importance. The Wine Museum in Palamós, for example, and the Wine and Cava Interpretation Center in Peralada, for example, both provide interactive exhibitions and tastings to help you learn more about and appreciate local wines.

When attending wine and cava tastings, it is essential to drink safely and have a designated driver or arrange for transportation if necessary. Discover the region's rich viticultural legacy and enjoy in wonderful tastes that represent the region's particular features by experiencing Costa Brava's wines and cavas.

CHAPTER 8: Festivals and Events in Costa Brava.

Costa Brava is a Catalan area with a lively cultural legacy, and one of the finest ways to appreciate this heritage is to participate in the traditional festivals that take place throughout the year. These celebrations of Catalan customs, music, dancing, and gastronomy are boisterous. Here are some typical Costa Brava festivals that you may consider attending:

Carnival (Carnaval): Carnival is a joyful season observed across Costa Brava in February or March. Towns and cities come alive during this season with colorful parades, street festivities, and costume competitions. The carnival is distinguished by colorful costumes, traditional music, and dance. It's a happy gathering that celebrates the region's communal spirit and cultural diversity.

Day of Sant Jordi (Da de Sant Jordi): Sant Jordi's Day, observed on April 23rd, is a one-of-a-kind holiday that blends the traditions of Valentine's Day and World Book Day. On this day, flower sellers and bookstands line the streets, and people exchange flowers and books as gifts of love and friendship. It's a lovely ode to literature, romance, and Catalan culture.

Festa Major is a traditional Catalan event celebrated in several towns and villages around the Costa Brava. Each town has its unique festival date, which generally occurs during the summer months. The Festa Major includes a variety of events such as processions, live music, traditional dances, fireworks, and street vendors. It's a terrific chance to immerse yourself in local culture while also enjoying the festival's vibrant atmosphere.

Castells: Castells, or human towers, are a powerful Catalan tradition that represents strength, collaboration, and communal spirit. During festivals and other occasions, groups of people stand on one other's shoulders to build human towers. The towers, which may be many storeys tall, are accompanied by traditional music and clapping. A castells performance is a one-of-a-kind and exhilarating event that exhibits Catalan culture.

Sea Processions: The Costa Brava coastal communities organize sea processions, dubbed as "Processó de la Sardana Martima," to honor the sea and fisherman. During these processions, adorned boats carry the figure of the local patron saint out to sea, escorted by a fleet of smaller vessels. Traditional music and prayers accompany the procession, providing a peaceful and meditative environment.

Fira de la Cervesa Artesana (Craft Beer Fair): Costa Brava is well-known for both traditional and contemporary events. The Craft Beer Fair, which is hosted in different places around the area, highlights the region's thriving craft beer culture. Visitors may sample specialty brews, listen to live music, and eat at food vendors serving local and foreign cuisine. It's a terrific chance to witness the combination of traditional Catalan culture and modern trends.

Festes de Gràcia (Girona): In late July, Girona, one of the largest cities in Costa Brava, holds the Festes de Gràcia, a week-long celebration. Live music performances, street parades, traditional dances, and a fireworks show are all part of the celebration. Girona's streets are magnificently decked, and the atmosphere is alive with excitement and enthusiasm.

Attending these traditional festivals enables you to experience Costa Brava's rich cultural history, interact with the local people, and create lasting memories of your trip to the area. To completely immerse yourself in Catalan culture, embrace the brilliant colors, sounds, and smells of these events.

Cultural and Art Events.

Costa Brava is well-known not just for its natural beauty and breathtaking coastline, but also for its thriving cultural and creative environment. Throughout the year, the area holds a range of cultural and art events that showcase the abilities of local artists while also commemorating Costa Brava's rich legacy. Here are some important cultural and artistic events in the region:

Temps de Flors (Girona): Temps de Flors is a flower festival held in Girona each year in May. Girona's streets, courtyards, and old buildings are decked with stunning flower displays and creative exhibits throughout this festival. It's an enthralling sight that mixes art, nature, and architecture to turn the city into a vibrant paradise.

Cap Roig Festival (Calella de Palafrugell): During the summer months, the Cap Roig Festival is held in the spectacular botanical gardens of Cap Roig in Calella de Palafrugell. This prominent music festival includes a worldwide roster of performers playing in a stunning outdoor setting overlooking the Mediterranean Sea. The Cap Roig Festival features a diverse range of musical genres, from classical music and opera to modern pop and rock acts.

Torroella de Montgr International Music event: The International Music Festival of Torroella de Montgr is an acknowledged classical music event conducted in the summer in the town of Torroella de Montgr. The festival gathers world-renowned artists who play in ancient settings such as the Church of Sant Gens and the Castle of Montgr. The schedule comprises orchestral concerts, chamber music performances, and recitals, providing music lovers with an enriching experience.

Peralada Castle Festival: During the summer months, the Peralada Castle Festival is held in the charming hamlet of Peralada, near Figueres. The festival mixes music, dance, opera, theater, and art in a stunning setting—Peralada Castle's grounds. Audiences may enjoy performances by globally known artists while immersing themselves in this cultural event's wonderful environment.

Gala Dal Castle in Pbol: The Gala Dal Castle in Pbol is a museum devoted to the great artist Salvador Dal's life and work. Throughout the year, the castle holds exhibits of Dal's artwork, including paintings, sculptures, and installations. The chambers, gardens, and grave of Gala Dal, Salvador Dal's wife, are open to visitors. It's a once-in-a-lifetime chance to explore the strange universe of one of the twentieth century's most significant painters.

Contemporary Art Galleries: The Costa Brava region is home to a plethora of contemporary art galleries that display the works of both local and international artists. Cities like Girona and Figueres are especially rich in art galleries, allowing tourists to explore varied creative styles and discover new talents.

Traditional Festivals: Many traditional festivals in Costa Brava have artistic aspects in addition to specialized culture and art activities. Carnival, Sant Jordi's Day, and Festa Major events, for example, often involve street performances, music, and dance, giving a unique combination of traditional customs and creative manifestations.

Attending these Costa Brava culture and art events enables you to interact with the region's dynamic creative community, enjoy its cultural legacy, and immerse yourself in a world of creativity and expression. It's a fantastic chance to extend your stay in Costa Brava and obtain a better grasp of its artistic and cultural value.

Bars and Nightclubs in Costa Brava.

Costa Brava has a dynamic nightlife scene with a wide range of pubs and nightclubs to satisfy all interests and inclinations. Costa

Brava offers something for everyone, whether you prefer a laid-back ambiance to have a few drinks or want to dance the night away. Here are some of the most popular pubs and nightclubs in the area:

Lloret de Mar is renowned for its bustling nightlife, which attracts partygoers from all over the globe. Avinguda Just Marlès is the primary nightlife district of Lloret de Mar, with a multitude of pubs and clubs. Tropics Lloret, Revolution Disco, and St. Trop Lloret are among the most popular venues. These venues provide a variety of music styles, including as pop songs, house, and Latin rhythms.

Tossa de Mar: Like Lloret de Mar, Tossa de Mar has a vibrant nightlife scene, but in a more casual atmosphere. The old town is the primary center for pubs and nightclubs, mainly around Carrer Portal and Carrer Sant Antoni. Bars such as El Faro, El Bocil, and El Bar del Corb provide a comfortable setting in which to have a few drinks and mingle with friends.

Girona: Girona boasts a wide variety of pubs and nightclubs to suit all preferences. Bar hopping is common in Plaça de la Independència and Carrer de la Cort Reial. Vadevins, L'Arcada, and L'Antiquari are examples of fashionable establishments. If you're looking for live music, El Vermutet and Café Gora often hold concerts by local bands and artists.s.

Platja d'Aro: Platja d'Aro is yet another vibrant nightlife hotspot on the Costa Brava. Avinguda S'Agaró, the main street, is lined with pubs and clubs that provide a variety of music genres and party moods. Chiringuito El Pirata, La Dolce Vita, and Arena Platja d'Aro are popular places to dance and drink till the wee hours of the morning.

Figueres: Known for its ties to Salvador Dal, Figueres also boasts a lively nightlife scene. Carrer Nou and its neighboring streets are home to a number of pubs and lounges where you may unwind after a long day. El Pati de l'Estrella and Jard del Rector provide a quiet atmosphere in which to relax with a beverage or a glass of wine.

When experiencing the Costa Brava nightlife, keep the following guidelines in mind:

Check the dress code: Some nightclubs may have a dress code, so dress correctly to prevent any problems at the entry.

Take care of your belongings: It's crucial to keep a watch on your possessions and avoid carrying precious goods needlessly, like with any nighttime environment.

Drink responsibly: Consume alcohol sensibly and stay within your boundaries. To guarantee your safety, always appoint a designated driver or utilize other modes of transportation.

The nightlife in Costa Brava is active and diversified, catering to a wide range of tastes and giving a chance to spend a fantastic evening out during your stay to the area.

Live Music and Cultural Performances.

Costa Brava is well-known not just for its natural beauty, but also for its thriving live music and cultural performance culture. The area has a variety of places and events where you may learn about local music and cultural customs. Here are some of our favorite picks for seeing live music and cultural acts in Costa Brava:

Concert Halls and Theaters: Cities such as Girona and Figueres have concert halls and theaters where a variety of performances are held throughout the year. The Teatre Municipal de Girona and the Teatre-Museu Dal in Figueres are both prominent venues for concerts, theater plays, and dance events by local and international performers.

Festivals of Traditional Music and Dance: Costa Brava is recognized for its rich cultural past, and many festivals honor traditional music and dance. The Girona Festival of Religious

Music offers sacred music concerts in old cathedrals, providing a unique and fascinating environment. Another famous event is the Festival de Msica de Cadaqués, which brings together renowned performers and orchestras for classical music concerts.

Street Performers: The lovely streets of Costa Brava are often bustling with street performers showing their abilities. In places like Girona and Tossa de Mar, singers, painters, and dancers amuse passerby with their talents. The historic cities' small alleyways create an intimate and energetic venue for spontaneous performances.

Cultural Centers and Museums: There are various cultural centers and museums on the Costa Brava that host events and performances. The Palau de Congressos de Girona presents a wide range of cultural events, including as music concerts, theatrical plays, and art exhibits. The Museu de la Mediterrània in Torroella de Montgr often holds concerts and other events commemorating the Mediterranean heritage.

Local Bars and Cafés: Many Costa Brava local bars and cafés provide live music performances, especially during the summer months. These small locations allow you to hear local singers and bands while sipping a drink or eating a meal. Look for posters or ask locals for suggestions on where to discover live music in the neighborhood.

Traditional Festivals: Music and dance performances are typically included as part of the festivities of Costa Brava's traditional festivals, such as Festa Major and Carnival. These vibrant events provide an immersive experience where you can observe traditional folk music and dance styles such as the Sardana, a classic Catalan dance.

Outdoor Concerts: Throughout the summer, towns and communities along the Costa Brava host outdoor concerts in public squares, parks, and gardens. These open-air concerts provide a relaxing and joyful environment in which to enjoy live music beneath the sky. Check the local event calendars for upcoming outdoor concerts in the area.

Attending live music performances and cultural events in Costa Brava provides a one-of-a-kind chance to engage with the local arts scene, learn about the region's cultural traditions, and make unforgettable memories. Immerse yourself in the colorful environment, admire the creativity of local artists, and enjoy Costa Brava's rich cultural legacy.

CONCLUSION.

Finally, Costa Brava is a wonderful place that provides a plethora of activities for all types of travelers. Costa Brava offers something for everyone, from its magnificent beaches and craggy coastline to its rich history, lively culture, and wonderful food. This location in northeastern Spain will surpass your expectations, whether you're looking for leisure, adventure, or cultural immersion.

We have studied the best sights, activities, lodgings, food alternatives, and practical suggestions throughout our travel guide to guarantee a wonderful and hassle-free vacation to Costa Brava. From Barcelona's prominent sites, such as the awe-inspiring Sagrada Familia and the creative paradise of Park Güell, to Girona's lovely medieval architecture and romantic Jewish Quarter, each place has its own distinct appeal and intrigue.

Continuing on, you will come across the intriguing town of Figueres, which is home to the famed Dal Theatre-Museum, where you can immerse yourself in Salvador Dal's strange universe. Tossa de Mar and Cadaqués, two gorgeous coastal villages, will fascinate you with their exquisite beaches, historic monuments, and artistic ties.

The rocky beauty of Cap de Creus Natural Park gives numerous chances for trekking, discovering coastal pathways, and marveling at the stunning views from the Cap de Creus Lighthouse. Meanwhile, adventurers may enjoy a variety of water activities along the stunning coastline, from snorkeling and scuba diving to kayaking and paddleboarding. To get a true sense of Costa Brava, try the local food, which features classic Catalan meals brimming with flavors and fresh ingredients. You will embark on a gastronomic trip that will satisfy your taste buds, from eating tapas in crowded food markets to enjoying seafood delights in beachside eateries.

As you travel around Costa Brava, remember to observe the local traditions and etiquette, respect the environment, and be safe at all times. For a pleasant and worry-free journey, learn the local language and bring the essential travel papers and insurance.

With a variety of lodging choices ranging from luxury resorts to budget-friendly hostels, you can find the ideal location to relax and recharge after a day of exploring.

Whether you're a history buff, a nature lover, an art enthusiast, or just want to relax in the Mediterranean heat, Costa Brava has a rich tapestry of experiences that will leave an indelible imprint. So pack your bags and prepare to be enchanted by Costa Brava's beauty, culture, and kind welcome. In this enthralling part of Spain, your adventure awaits.

Printed in Great Britain
by Amazon

28140453R00076